AF580354

ARID WATERS

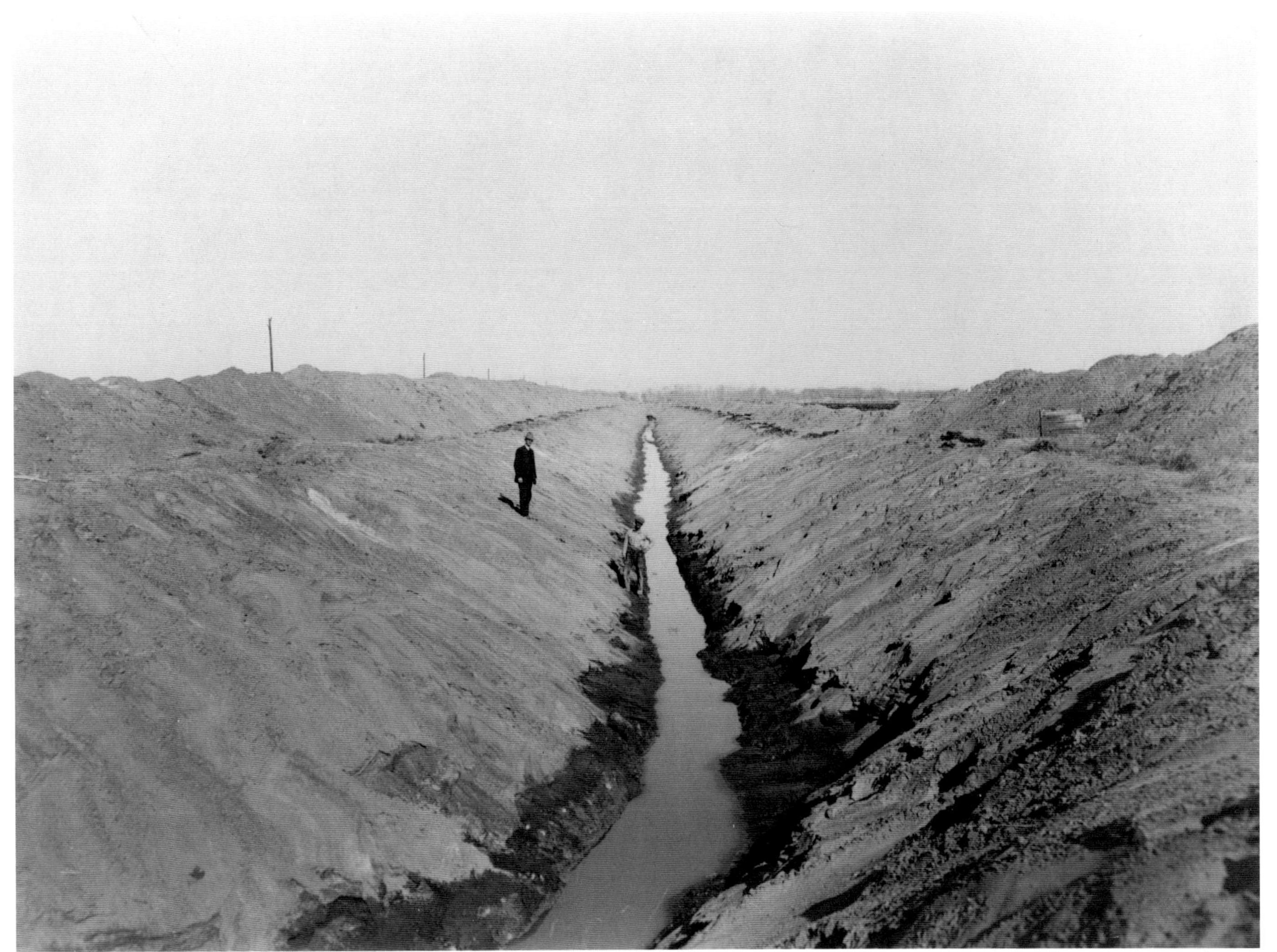

ARID WATERS

Photographs from the Water in the West Project. Edited by Peter Goin. Text by Ellen Manchester

UNIVERSITY OF NEVADA PRESS ▲▲ RENO, LAS VEGAS & LONDON

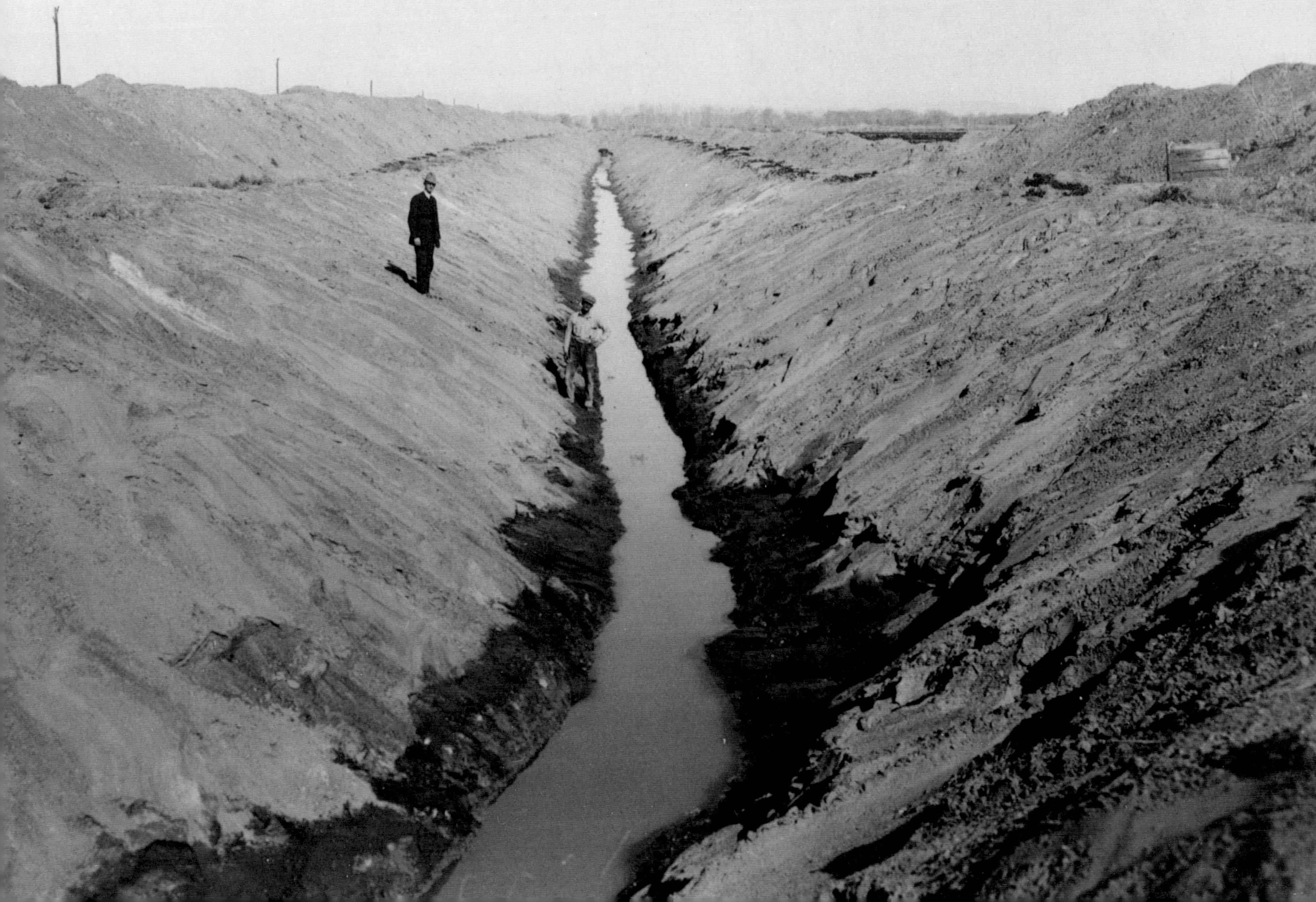

This project was made possible by generous support from:
University of Nevada, Reno Academic Affairs
Sierra Arts Foundation
Nevada Humanities Committee
University of Nevada, Reno Foundation

The paper used in this book meets the requirements of American National Standard for Information Sciences—Permanence of Paper for Printed Library Materials, ANSI Z39.48–1984. Binding materials were selected for strength and durability.

University of Nevada Press, Reno, Nevada 89557 USA

Book design by Richard Hendel
Printed in the United States of America
9 8 7 6 5 4 3 2 1

Library of Congress Cataloging-in-Publication Data
Arid waters : photographs from the Water in the West Project / edited by Peter Goin ; text by Ellen Manchester.
p. cm.
Includes bibliographical references (p.)
ISBN 0-87417-198-9 (cloth) ISBN 0-87417-199-7 (paper ed.)
1. Water-supply—West (U.S.)—Exhibitions. 2. Water use—West (U.S.)—Exhibitions. 3. Hydraulic structures—West (U.S.)—Exhibitions. I. Goin, Peter, 1951– . II. Manchester, Ellen. III. Sheppard Fine Art Gallery.
TD223.6.A84 1992
333.91'2'0978022—dc20 92-20023
CIP

TITLE PAGE

Truckee Canal, part of the Truckee-Carson Irrigation Project, later named the Newlands Irrigation Project. This project was the first federal attempt at irrigating desert lands by diverting water from its river source, ca. 1905. Courtesy of the Special Collections Department, University of Nevada, Reno, Library.

CONTENTS

PROLOGUE

The Water in the West Project is a photographic response to the growing water crisis that exists because our culture thinks of water as a commodity, or an abstract legal right, rather than the most basic physical source of life. The Water in the West exhibit was held at the Sheppard Fine Art Gallery in the Art Department at the University of Nevada, Reno, from April 25 through June 16, 1991. This exhibit was also the occasion of the third meeting of the Water in the West Project, and it was intended to serve as a catalyst for the collaborating photographers to identify the most effective and appropriate role for their work in public debate. (The first two meetings were held at the Headlands Center for the Arts in Marin, north of San Francisco, and the fourth meeting and exhibit was held at the Land Institute in Salina, Kansas, in October 1991.)

Instead of a loose association of artists simply interested in issues provoked by water scarcity, the Water in the West Project planned to use the meeting in Reno as an opportunity to realize selected common objectives. First, Ellen Manchester and the photographers—Mark Klett, Terry Evans, Laurie Brown, Robert Dawson, Martin Stupich, Gregory Conniff, Wanda Hammerbeck, and myself—wanted to begin answering the question: How can photography contribute to the urgent public debate over water use, allocation, and privilege? Many people believe that art's primary function is to entertain or decorate, yet photography is uniquely qualified to offer information and visual insight. Thus, a primary objective of the Water in the West Project became the establishment of an archive and expansion of the potential for interdisciplinary work.

Second, recognizing that art is often subjected to the sanitizing influence of a gallery's white walls, the Water in the West Project wanted to reinterpret the role of the gallery. The exhibition of finished, matted, and framed work was minimized in favor of work-in-progress. Although forty-eight feet of wall space were allocated for finished works, over one hundred feet became a bulletin board of selected documents, narrative sequences, combination prints, contact sheets, and multiple images. The Sheppard Fine Art Gallery became more of a laboratory than a museum as the *process* of working through ideas became emphasized.

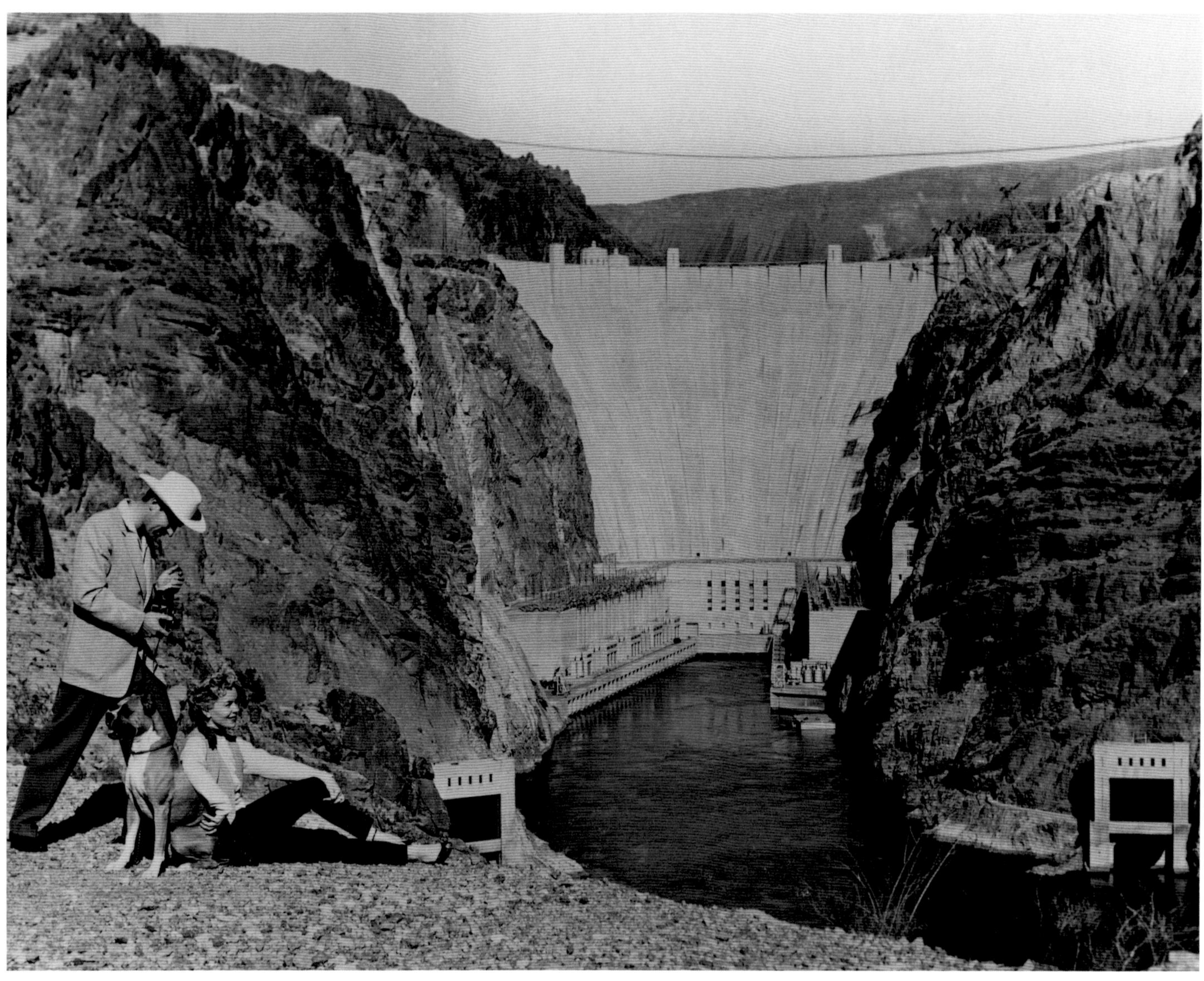

PHOTOGRAPHER UNIDENTIFIED. LAS VEGAS NEWS BUREAU PHOTO

2. "CONCRETE GIANT—Hoover (Boulder) Dam is the highest dam in the world and forms Lake Mead, the largest man-made lake in the world, from the turbulent Colorado River dividing Arizona and Nevada. The concrete giant is also a bridge for U.S. Highways 93 and 466, two of the main cross-country highways. Located 30 miles from Las Vegas, Nevada, Hoover Dam has attracted more than 6,000,000 visitors since its completion in 1936." Original caption from back of print. Courtesy of the Special Collections Department, University of Nevada, Reno, Library.

At the same time, the Nevada Humanities Committee sponsored a conference entitled "Water in the Arid West," and historians, writers, ranchers, politicians, lawyers, students, and community members participated. Panel discussions and lectures were held in the gallery, and a new audience was introduced to the merger of art and issue-oriented debate about water. The photographers and selected scholars met in a publicly attended round-table discussion, creating a unique opportunity for intellectual sharing. The photographs displayed at the gallery—many more than would be expected given the available space—provided ample evidence and a constant reminder of the relevance of visual information and interpretation.

Students from the Art Department curated an exhibit of historical photographs from the Newlands Irrigation Project, the first federal water reclamation effort in the West (1906), and contrasted these photographs with Las Vegas publicity stills advertising the appearance of an abundance of water in the desert. This exhibit was installed in the SXN Gallery, essentially the main hallway leading to the Sheppard Gallery. (The historical photographs came from the Special Collections Department, University of Nevada, Reno, Library; the cover image is one of the more than fifty photographs exhibited.) Thirty-five photographs from the Water in the West Project were included in the Nevada Humanities Committee anthology of writings on water issues, *A River Too Far* (Reno: University of Nevada Press, 1991).

This exhibit and publication are the first public programming specifically sponsored by the Water in the West Project. Project members are deeply concerned about the relationship of water to culture and hope to exercise our rights and obligations as citizens by producing this art. I know that the sponsoring institutions—Sierra Arts Foundation, Nevada Humanities Committee, and the University of Nevada, Reno—share with us our desire to integrate art photography, dialogue, public debate, and education. The selfless support of the many individuals that helped make the meetings, conference, and publication possible has given me the optimism to report that art does, indeed, matter.

Peter Goin

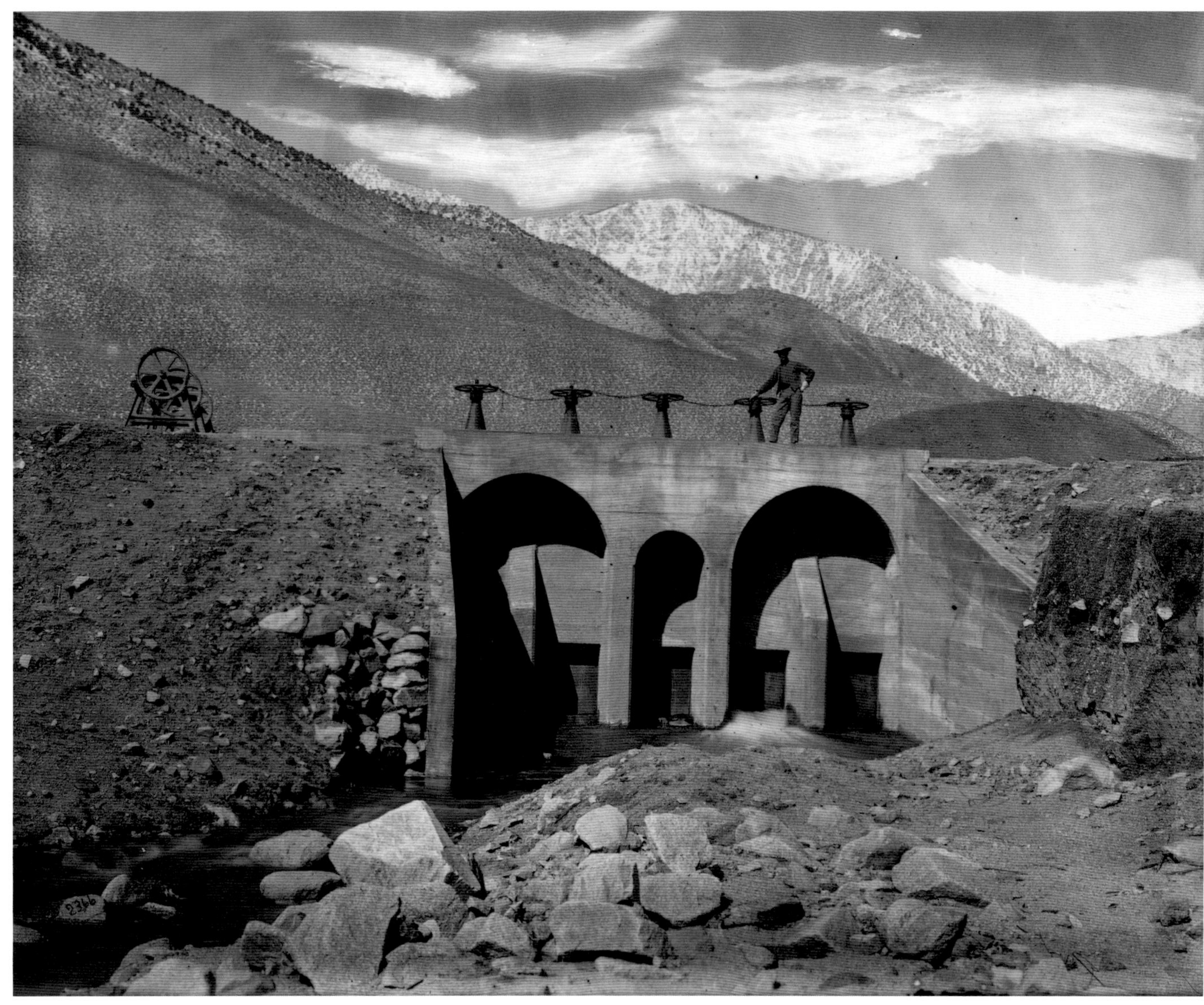

JAMES BLEDSOE

3. The Alabama Gates of the First Los Angeles Aqueduct, ca. 1913. The Alabama Gates in California's Owens Valley controlled the flow of water into the first aqueduct built to deliver water to the city of Los Angeles. In 1924, the seizure of these gates and the earlier dynamiting of the aqueduct by angry Owens Valley residents was part of a bitter battle between the Los Angeles Department of Water and Power and Owens Valley. Courtesy of Public Affairs Division, Los Angeles Department of Water and Power.

ARID WATERS

When Samuel Coleridge's ancient mariner was cast adrift at sea he cried: "Water, water everywhere, nor any drop to drink." The irony in the American West today is that we have *no* water, yet *seem* to have plenty to drink. The West is in the midst of a severe drought, having endured less than 75 percent of "normal" rainfall levels over the past six years. Yet we continue to build new homes in arid lands, water lawns and fill swimming pools in our cities, build desert resorts with indoor tropical rainforests, and grow rice and cotton in flood-irrigated fields. The present-day water scarcity will have a profound impact on future generations.

Water has become wealth, and its ostentatious display is an ironic reminder of its scarcity. Artificial lakes, vista ponds, and flowering fountains create the illusion that water is plentiful. But water is not plentiful when measured against the ever-increasing demands of corporate agribusiness, artificial environments, and urban growth. Water is being drawn out of the ground at a much faster rate than it can be replenished. Clouds are being seeded with the hope of increasing rainfall. Complex plans for "water-grabbing" are being developed throughout the arid West on a daily basis. Clearly, our needs are out of balance with the natural supply of this most vital resource.

Water has always been the essential element in sustaining human life. No ranch, Indian settlement, way station, military outpost, or business center could have come about without readily available water. Nor could the land have supported the extensive urban development, mining, agriculture, and tourist and recreation industries that have exploded in the West over the past 140 years without access to massive quantities of water. The control, management, and exploitation of water, more than any other resource in the West, has dramatically changed the shape of the natural and social landscape of this region.

These western lands have been thoroughly surveyed, mapped, bulldozed, blasted, and reshaped to meet both the real and imagined needs of the Anglo-European peoples that have settled here. Rivers have been dammed, rerouted, straightened, and even made to run uphill. Parts of great rivers such as the Colorado, the Snake, and the Arkansas cease to flow at certain times of year due to oversubscription upstream by agriculture and urban development. Lakes and ponds have disappeared as water is sucked from their inflow streams, while elsewhere, massive reservoirs now cover some of the country's most majestic canyons and valleys.

Water quality is now as complex an issue as its scarcity. Valuable wetlands and marshes, habitat for many species of birds and animals, have dried up or are dangerously polluted. Fish and wildlife in places such as California's Kesterson Wildlife Refuge and Colorado's Arkansas River are constantly subjected to high levels of heavy metals leaching from adjacent agricultural fields and mines. Fishing, the economic lifeblood of many Indian tribes, has all too often been decimated due to diverted streams, dammed rivers, drastically fluctuating water levels in rivers and lakes, and pollution from nearby industry and agriculture.

The story of water in the West is the story of a culture embracing and perpetuating nineteenth-century beliefs in the myth of the boundless frontier, idealized nature, unlimited resources, and unrestrained individual freedoms—there would always be new territories to explore, new rivers to tap, new gold veins to mine, and remote wilderness areas where one could escape the increasing pressures of urban life. One needs only to look at the rapid urbanization of desert cities such as Phoenix, Los Angeles, Reno, and Las Vegas, the verdant golf courses in Palm Springs, minimally regulated open-pit mining, and dirt bikes tearing across fragile sand dunes to see examples of how these beliefs, and the value systems upon which they were built, still dominate our relationship to the western landscape.

Water, like nature, has become a commodity. Water recreation has been aggressively developed, with water parks, Bureau of Reclamation reservoirs, and wild rivers further exploiting water as an industry unto itself. In the middle of the Arizona desert, water parks with "ocean" surf have become popular. Water has been objectified and defined as "the other"—something that is separate from us and therefore not an integral part of our relationship to, and dependence upon, the natural ecosystem. Our lives have become so far removed from water's source that we no longer see the direct connection between water as an element of nature and turning on the tap. It is this separateness that reinforces the exploitation of water. Because of this, we have also lost touch with the spiritual, metaphorical, symbolic, and life-sustaining aspects of water. As historian Donald Worster points out, our society has lost its respect for water as anything other than a raw commodity:

> Water in our present economy has no intrinsic value, no integrity that must be respected. Water is no longer valued as a divinely appointed means for survival, for producing and reproducing human life, as it was in ancient societies. Nor is water an awe-inspiring, animistic ally in a quest for political empire, as it was in the agrarian states. It has now become a commodity that is bought and sold and used to make other commodities that can be bought and sold and carried to the marketplace. It is, in other words, purely and abstractly a commercial instrument. All mystery disappears from its depth, all gods depart, all contemplation of its flow ceases. It becomes so many "acre-feet" banked in an account, so many "kilowatt-hours" of generating capacity to be spent, so many bales of cotton or carloads of oranges to be traded around the globe. And in that new language of market calculation lies an assertion of ultimate power over nature—of a domination that is absolute, total, and free from all restraint.[1]

To the members of the Water in the West Project, water is the most compelling metaphor and prescient symbol for the legacy of attitudes that have so profoundly shaped the landscape of the West. The full range of our nation's regard for the natural world has manifest itself in western water history—from loving stewardship and respect to outrageous abuse and plunder. The Water in the West Project is studying the cultural values and attitudes that have brought us to this critical imbalance with nature. Through researching historical images and creating contemporary photographs, the project's goal is to create a collection of photographs and related visual materials that will contribute significantly to the dialogue about the future and quality of life on earth as sustained by increasingly limited natural resources such as water. The project will serve as a clearinghouse for ideas and as a structure to encourage collaborative and interdisciplinary work on critical cultural and environmental issues through the establishment of a comprehensive archive of both historical and contemporary photographs, through public lectures and symposia, and through a continuing series of publications and exhibitions.

Although the current water crisis may be global, the Water in the West Project has chosen to focus on the American West, for it is here that the impact of human settlement and resource development on arid lands is most visible. The project is currently concerned with the region extending from the western plains to the California coast, and from the basin areas of eastern Washington and Oregon to the Mexican border. This region, which encompasses the Great Basin, the Rocky Mountains, the Sierra Nevada, and much of the Great Plains, commonly receives less than twenty inches of precipitation annually (the amount considered necessary for nonirrigated farming) and is frequently subjected to extended periods of drought.

Nineteenth-century photographers provided some of the earliest visual accounts of the landscape and inhabitants of the West. The photograph, although often promoted as a document free of artistic embellishments and pictorial conventions, was inextricably bound to the cultural beliefs, artistic fashions, and political climate of the period. The spirit of Manifest Destiny and its aggressive western expansionism, pictorial conventions of the sublime, idyllic landscape learned in European academies, and the myth of the romantic hero/mountainman in the wilderness influenced the artistic and photographic interpretation of the West as a place of monumental landscapes, exotic beauty, and of wildness to be tamed.

Reproductions and accounts in popular journals of the day trace the earliest photographic efforts to document the Great Plains, Rocky Mountain, and Great Basin regions to J. Wesley Jones's expedition of 1851, only twelve years after the official invention of photography in France. Although no actual plates are known to exist, Jones claims to have made more than 1,500 daguerreotypes in the region. The unwieldy daguerreotype process was also used by artist Solomon N. Carvalho when he accompanied Colonel John Frémont on his final expedition to the western territories in 1853.

Carvalho's account of photographing from a Colorado mountaintop provides a glimpse of the attitudes these artists brought with them from the East Coast, but reveals surprisingly little about the ordeal of making daguerreotypes standing in snow up to his waist with temperatures often plunging to 20 and 30 degrees below zero.

> After three hours' hard toil we reached the summit and beheld a panorama of unspeakable sublimity spread out before us; continuous chains of mountains reared their snowy peaks far away in the distance, while the Grand River [now the Colorado] plunging along in awful sublimity through its rocky bed, was seen for the first time. Above us the cerulean heaven, without a single cloud to mar its beauty, was sublime in its calmness. Plunged up to my middle in snow, I made a panorama of the continuous ranges of mountains around us.[2]

After the Civil War the country was anxious for a new national identity and systematically sought it in the monumental landscape beyond the Mississippi and Missouri rivers. Photographers accompanied each of the four major government surveys undertaken between 1867 and 1879, the year that the various efforts were consolidated to form the United States Geological Survey. These large-scale projects brought together teams of geologists, engineers, biologists, military experts, archaeologists, cartographers, and artists to describe and define the uncharted western territories. Some focused on the water and economic potential of the land, mapping out river systems, possible reservoir sites, ore deposits, and lumber acreage. Some emphasized the exotic beauty of the Rocky Mountains, the arid desert canyons, and the bizarre natural phenomena of remote places such as the geysers and hot springs of Yellowstone country. Others focused on the natural history and archaeology of the region, producing elegant albums of exquisite full-color lithographs of the flora, fauna, and archaeological findings of the expedition. Still others plotted future transportation systems for the efficient mobilization of military troops north, south, east, and west across the country. (Many of these routes have become the basis for the interstate highway system as we know it today.) The photographs resulting from these explorations became part of each survey's annual report and were widely exhibited at expositions and centennial fairs. They were also published in limited-edition albums, as reproductions in popular journals, and as stereo views. Stereo views were small photographs that when viewed through a special holder produced a three-dimensional "lifelike" image. Sold as sets, one could subscribe to a series and invite friends over to be armchair travelers through the Colorado Rockies, the

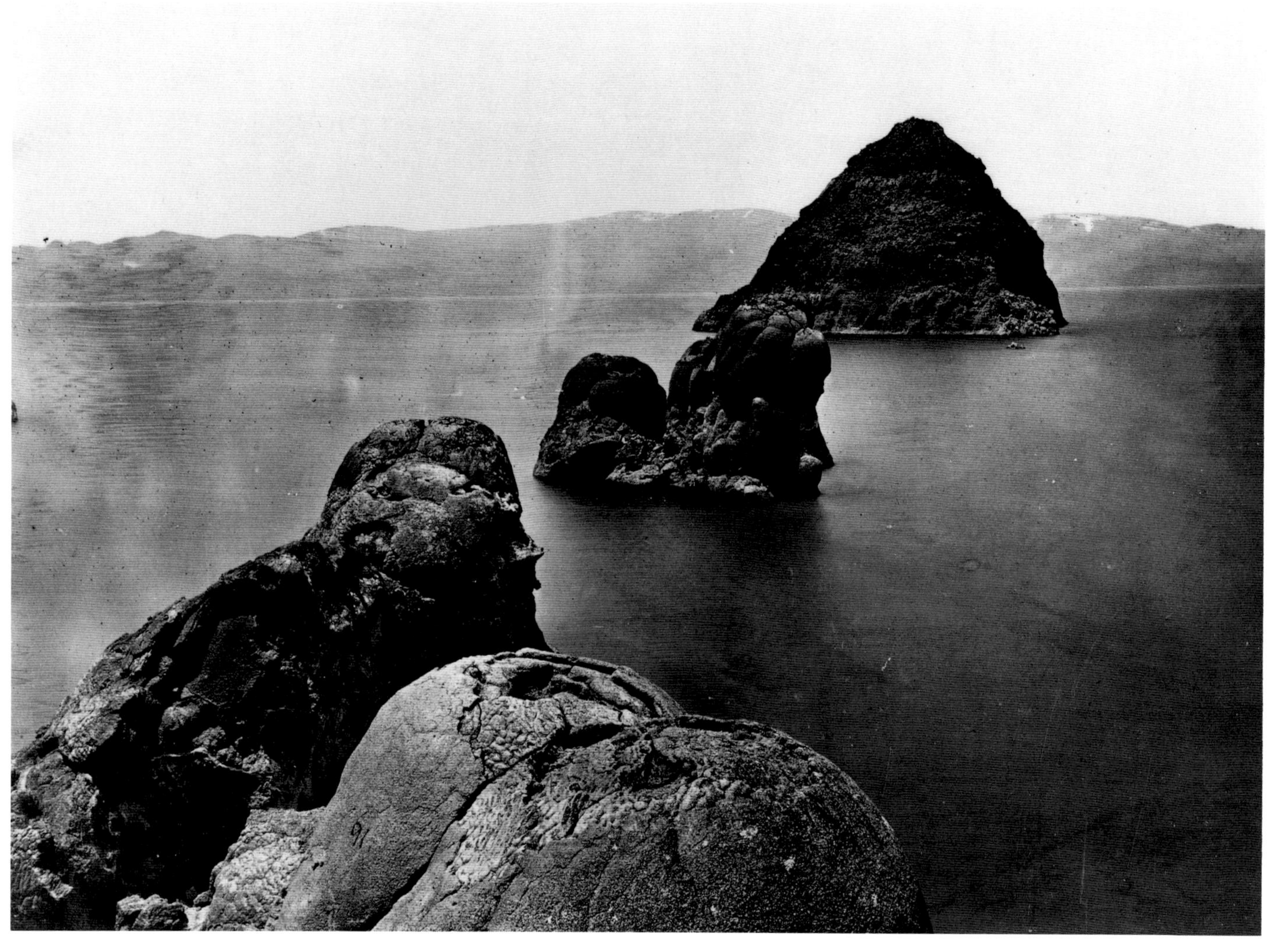

TIMOTHY O'SULLIVAN

4A. Rock Formations, Pyramid Lake, Nevada, 1867. Courtesy of Massachusetts Institute of Technology.

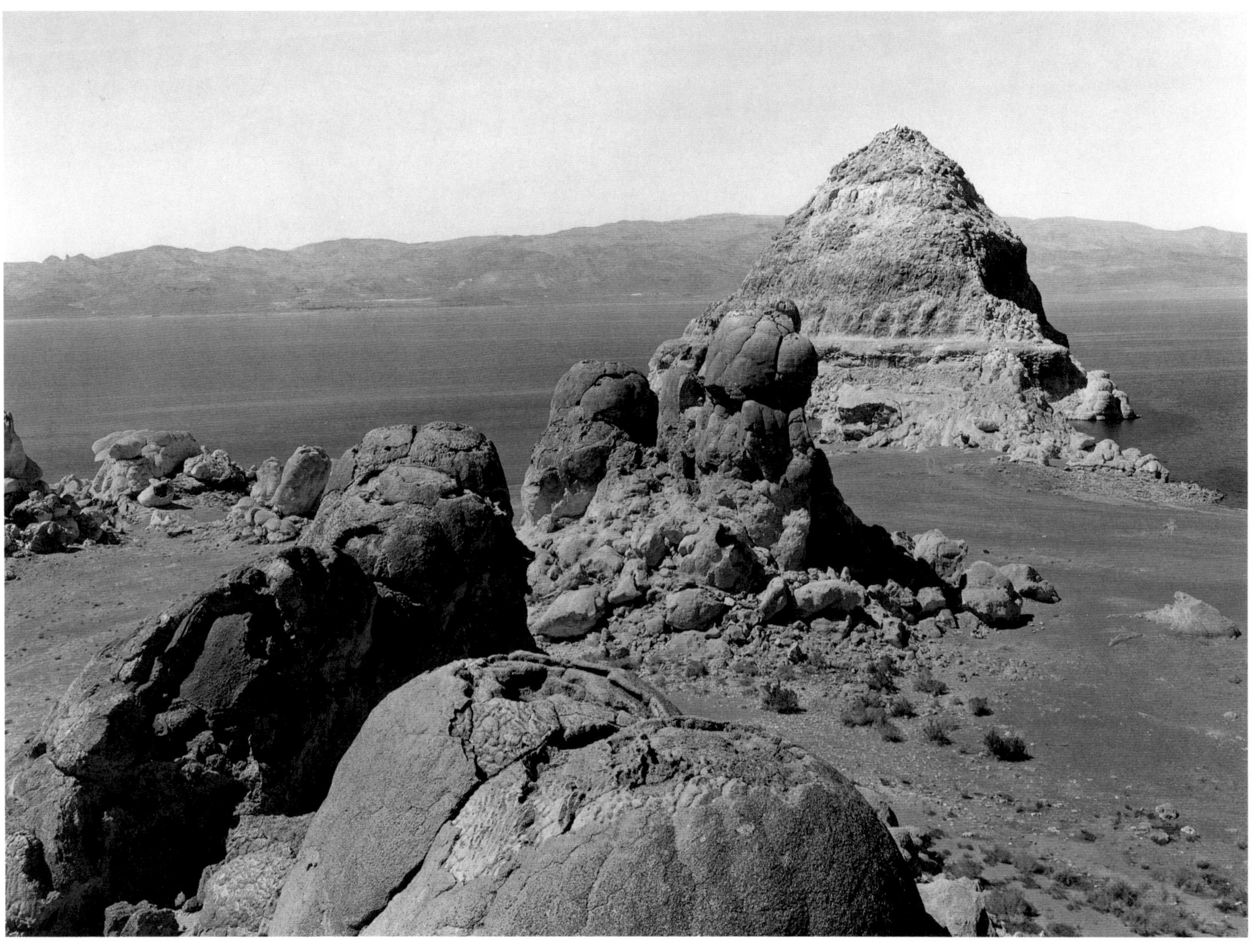

MARK KLETT FOR THE REPHOTOGRAPHIC SURVEY PROJECT

4B. Pyramid Lake, Nevada, 1979. Comparison shows the dramatic drop in water level due to diversion of Truckee River waters for urban and agricultural use near Reno and Sparks, combined with several years of drought. Courtesy of the Rephotographic Survey Project.

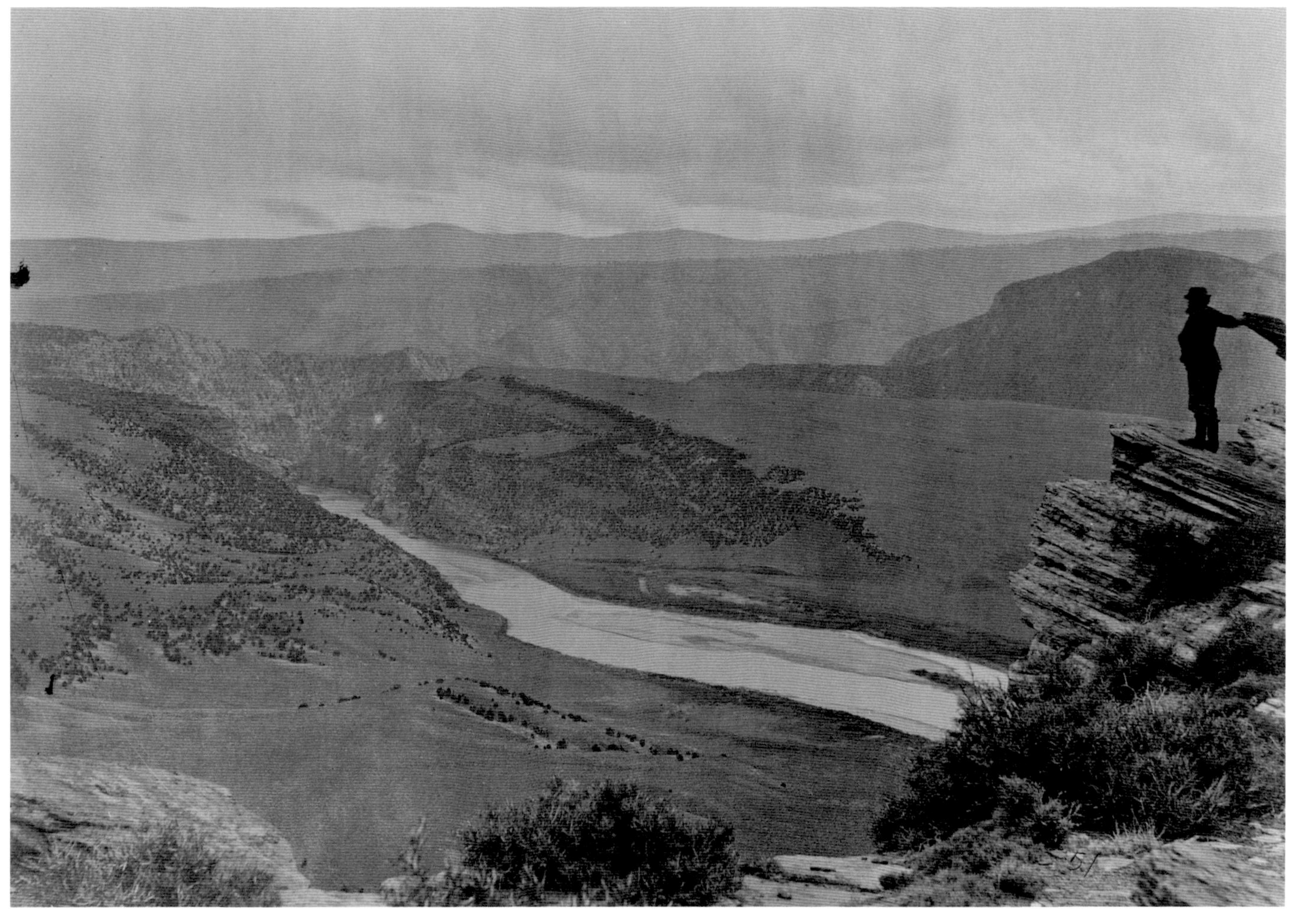

TIMOTHY O'SULLIVAN

4c. Green River Cañons, Upper Cañon, Great Bend, Green River below Horseshoe Bend from Flaming Gorge Cliff, 1872.

Courtesy of the United States Geological Survey, Denver.

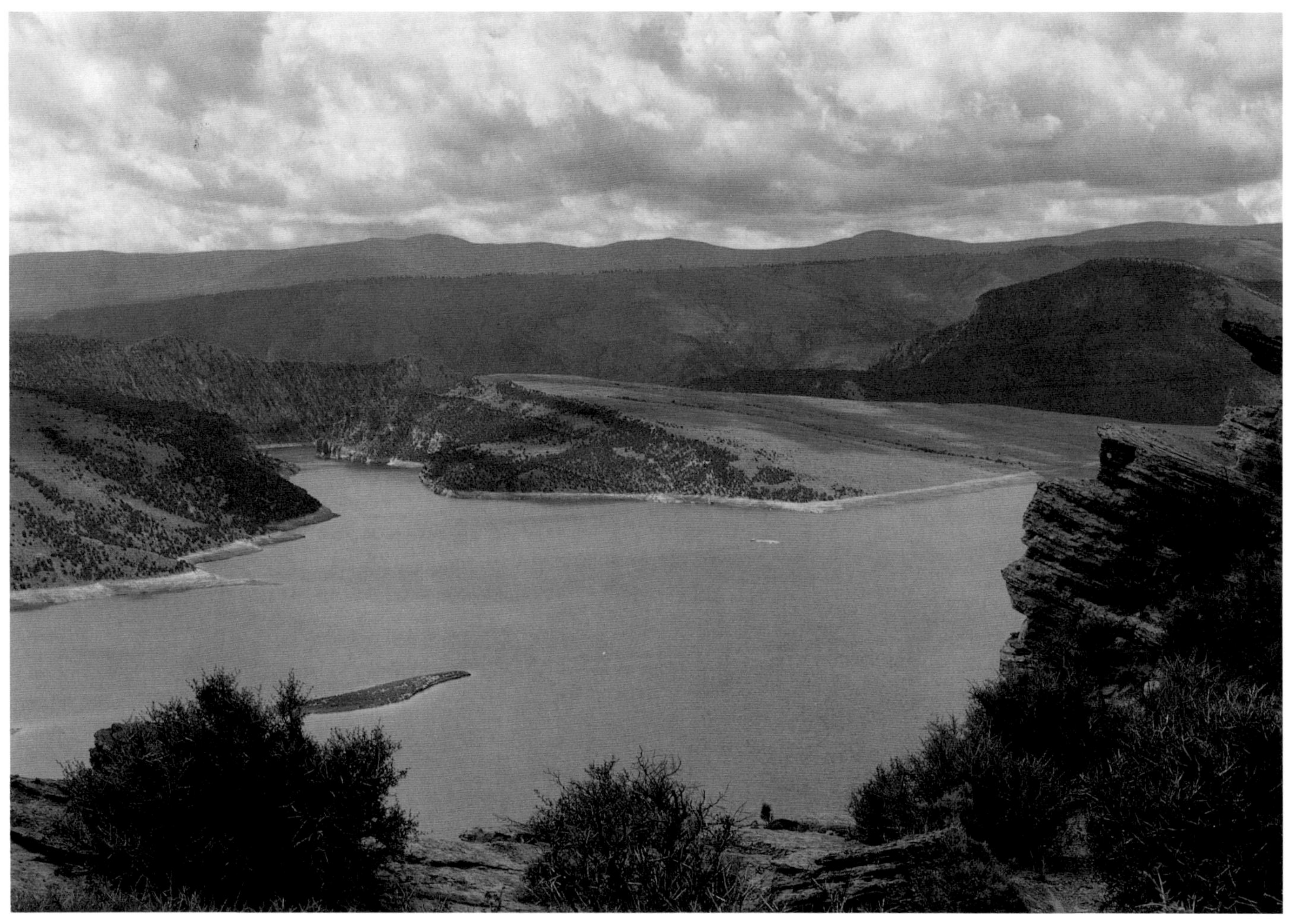

MARK KLETT FOR THE REPHOTOGRAPHIC SURVEY PROJECT

4D. Green River Reservoir looking south, Utah, 1978. Comparison shows reservoir built on site surveyed in 1872 by the Geological Explorations of the 40th Parallel under the direction of Clarence King. Courtesy of the Rephotographic Survey Project.

grand canyons of the southwest, the mining districts of Nevada, or other regions of natural beauty. The public enthusiastically embraced the absolute veracity of the photograph, even in the form of magazine reproductions—of an artist's interpretation—of the original photograph. To a country ripped apart by war, with little appreciated cultural history and few architectural treasures, these photographs of the West began to describe a nation of awesome strength, sublime beauty, boundless frontiers, and unlimited natural resources. These images, which had such a strong influence on how the public perceived the West in the nineteenth century, still dominate our sense of the western landscape today.

The first survey photographer to go west after the war was Timothy O'Sullivan. He was hired to accompany Clarence King's U.S. Geological Exploration of the Fortieth Parallel in 1867 and continued to work for both King and Lieutenant George Wheeler's U.S. Geographical Survey of the Territory West of the 100th Meridian until 1874. Today, O'Sullivan's photographs are often regarded as some of the most visually compelling and original work from the period. Unlike many of the other photographers of his time, O'Sullivan's work has a persuasive documentary nature and looks more like scientific data. Historians believe that his vision was not as constrained or influenced by prevailing nineteenth-century painterly conventions as were other photographers of his day (although we do know that he took quite a few "artistic liberties" with his images, often tilting the camera to exaggerate the tilt of a rock formation, or pasting in a mask to create a harsh, white-hot sky). His fascination for the awesome and terrible beauty of the desert is no doubt a reflection of the views of catastrophic geology held by King and other survey party members. O'Sullivan, like many of the other survey photographers, however, also focused on the rapid industrialization of the West as seen in his extensive documentation of mining activities throughout Nevada.

Photographer William Henry Jackson joined geologist Ferdinand Vandiveer Hayden on his survey of the Yellowstone territories in 1871 and 1872 and continued to work with Hayden's Geographical and Geological Surveys of the Territories for the next seven years. Jackson, who at one point worked side by side with the painter Thomas Moran, relied heavily on romantic pictorial conventions of the period to create his dramatic images of the new West. Hayden recognized the persuasive power of the photograph as a political tool and utilized Jackson's spectacular images in the successful plea to Congress to establish Yellowstone as the first national park in 1872. The legacy of Jackson's work is so strong that, today, in Yellowstone "picture spots" or site markers are placed at the exact spot from which he made his original photograph. His photographs, encased in plastic at each site, literally direct how we, as visitors, experience that landscape today. The view, and the experience, become validated and even sanctified as the "best general view." Jackson's influence can also be traced directly to the work of Ansel Adams and other Sierra Club photographers whose images have embraced and perpetuated the nineteenth-century romantic vision of idealized nature. The Sierra Club's innovative exhibition-format books, under the direction of David Brower, established an important precedent for utilizing the photograph as a political tool to lobby for environmental issues.

The work of many other nineteenth-century photographers has influenced how we perceive the West today. Paintings derived from photographs, reproductions in journals, stereo views, postcards taken from the same camera location, and travel brochures made extensive use of work by photographers such as E. O. Beaman and John K. Hillers, who joined John Wesley Powell in his expeditions down the Colorado and throughout the southwest; William Bell, who worked with the Wheeler survey; Carleton Watkins and Eadweard Muybridge, whose work focused on Yosemite, the Sierra Nevada range, and mining in California and Nevada; and Andrew J. Russell, noted Civil War photographer, who was commissioned to document the construction of the Union Pacific Railroad.

The influence of these photographers can be seen in the current work of many of the artists in the Water in the West Project. Mark Klett's work in the lower Colorado River Basin continually reflects upon western history and how it has dominated our experience of landscape.[3] Klett often incorporates a specific reference to the photographs of O'Sullivan, Bell, or Hillers into his images. Wanda Hammerbeck's large-scale color desert landscapes owe much to the provocatively quiet vision of O'Sullivan's grand views. Peter Goin's austere images of the Great Basin and "ghost landscapes" of the nuclear industry comment with irony on both Jackson and O'Sullivan's fascination with the industrialization—and sublime beauty—of the West.[4] Robert Dawson's images of tourist spots, mining towns, and river systems of the Rockies and Sierras visually refer to the earlier work of Jackson and O'Sullivan and challenge the "boom and bust" mentality that has formed these places.[5] Carleton Watkins's photographs of California agriculture and mining certainly had a strong influence on Dawson's Central Valley Project work. Laurie Brown's expansive panoramic scenes were influenced by the nineteenth-century landscape "view." Martin Stupich's panoramic images of large-scale mining and engineering works reflect back to the precise documentation of public and private enterprise by Watkins, Jackson, and O'Sullivan. Terry Evans's photographs of her homeland in western Kansas bring an intimate and lyrical perspective to the traditional nineteenth-century depiction of the Great Plains as rugged frontier.[6]

In the history of American photography, the New York Film and Photo League, the Farm Security Administration (FSA) surveys, and the National Endowment for the Arts Photography Survey Grants have served as important models for the concept and structure of the Water in the West Project. In many of these cases, the photograph was viewed as an educational tool and as a vehicle for informing the public about social and political ideas. In studying other collaborative surveys, the members of the Water in the West Project are looking at how each was organized; what the role was of the artist/photographer in shaping the direction and goals of the project; what the relationship was of the artist's individual aesthetic to the collection of raw visual data; how cultural and historical attitudes and events influenced the resulting photographs; whether there was a single, coherent voice and whether work and goals changed over time; who the audience was for the work; how the photographs reached the public; whether there was a clear understanding of the context for the work; whether the artists had a strong political voice and, if so, whether their work actually brought about significant social change; and how their work is accessible to historians and researchers today.

The New York Film and Photo League, founded in 1928, was a collaborative effort by a group of artists to promote documentary photography as a tool for social change. Photographers Sid Grossman and Sol Libsohn organized photographers to document aspects of urban life in New York. In 1936 the filmmakers broke away from the group that then became the Photo League. Berenice Abbott's "Changing New York" and Aaron Siskind's "Harlem Document" are two of the most significant photographic projects to come out of the group. While the league embraced a wide range of photographic styles, a struggle continued between proponents of the pure document and those individuals whose work was of a more personal and creative nature. Some photographers felt that the photograph as a tool for political comment and social change should not be clouded with issues of aesthetics, design, and personal vision. Others, such as Paul Strand, led a shift toward emphasizing aesthetics, feeling that a strong artistic statement enhanced the power of the image to communicate. The league's interest in social issues eventually caused it to be viewed with great suspicion. Many of its members were blacklisted or taunted as Communists, and in 1951 political pressures forced the demise of the group. The Photo League attempted to tap the potential of the photograph as a tool for social change, yet what is revealing is how the group dealt with issues such as the relationship between aesthetics and fact, the artist's right to retain individual vision within the construct of a large project, and how the members worked collaboratively to set policy and determine the direction of their organization. The importance of the Photo League as a model for the Water in the West Project lies in the fact that photographers with diverse intellectual and creative styles sought common ground to address social concerns.

One of the most extensive photographic surveys in the history of photography was conducted by the Farm Security Administration in the 1930s. Part of President Roosevelt's New Deal, the FSA project grew out of the Resettlement Administration's efforts to document the plight of sharecroppers and tenant farmers who had been displaced by the Depression and to promote the benefits of federal assistance to the rural poor. Roy Stryker was hired in 1935 to direct the Historical Division of the FSA. Stryker had used photography in his sociology work at Columbia University and recognized the power of the photograph as a tool for social commentary. Under Stryker's direction, the project soon grew to be a comprehensive catalogue of rural life in America in the 1930s. Stryker hired highly skilled artists such as Dorothea Lange, Walker Evans, Arthur Rothstein, Russell Lee, Marion Post Wolcott, and Ben Shahn to carry out his assignments. Although Stryker wielded a strong hand in the direction of the project (he often sent photographers into the field with specific shooting scripts), he was open to new ideas and images that the artists sent from their travels across the country. The project evolved over the years as the photographers' work began to challenge preconceptions about life in rural America. While the artists' personal vision and working style often clashed with Stryker's needs for the project, many of the photographers were able

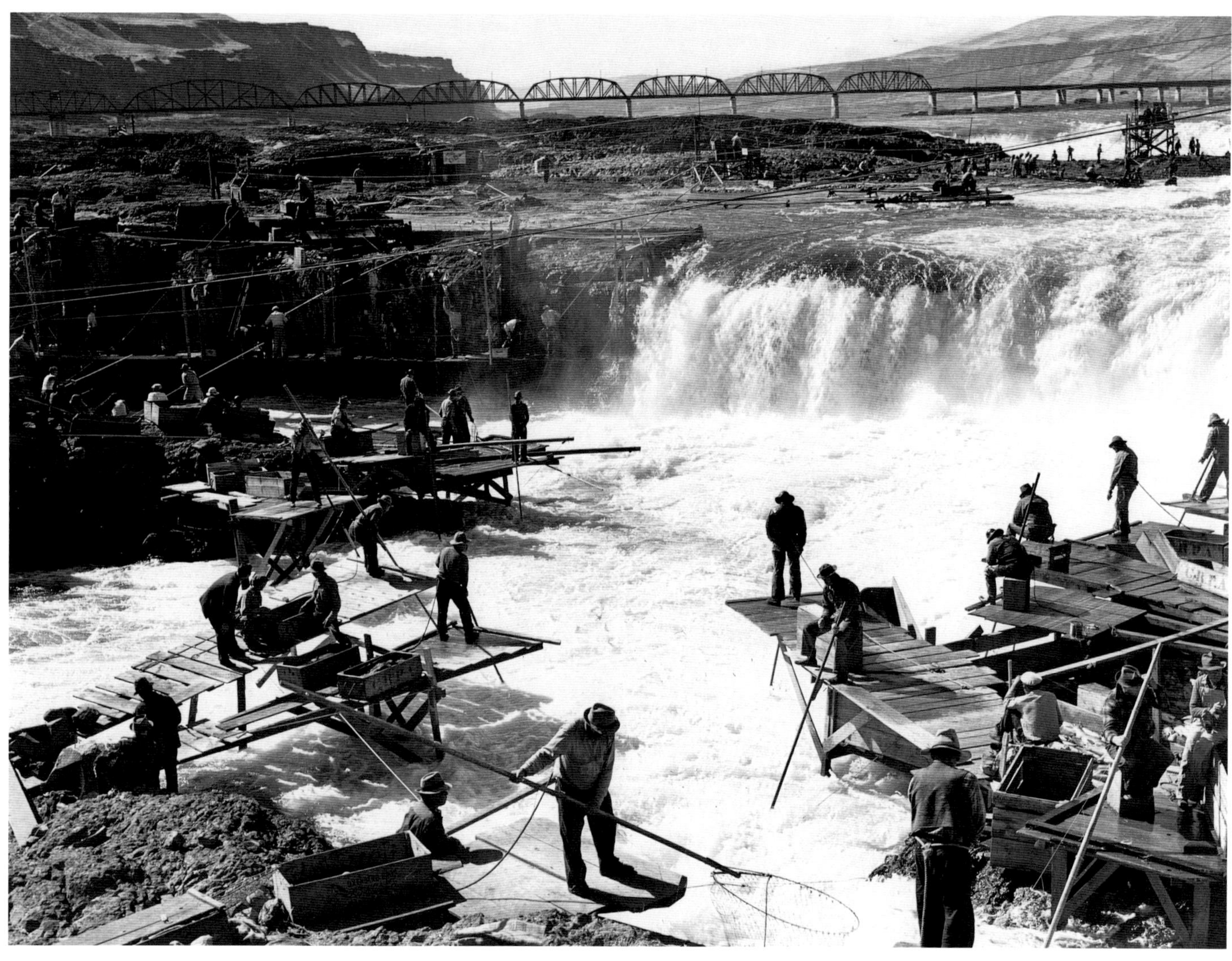

RUSSELL LEE FOR THE FARM SECURITY ADMINISTRATION

5. Native Americans fishing at Celilo Falls, Columbia River, Oregon, 1941. The site of Bonneville Dam, this area is now flooded. Courtesy of the Library of Congress.

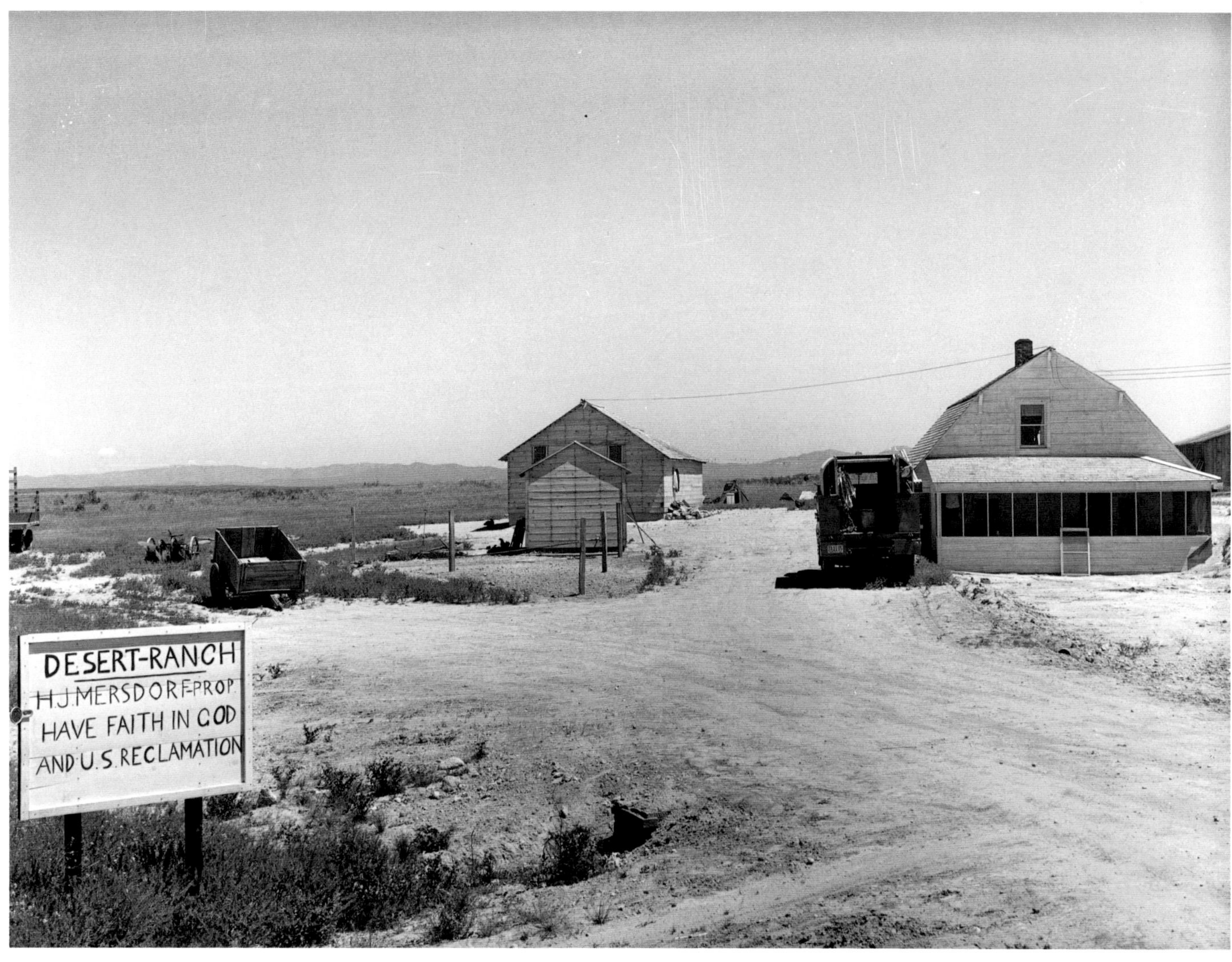

RUSSELL LEE FOR THE FARM SECURITY ADMINISTRATION

6. "Canyon County, Idaho. June 1941. A desert ranch whose owner is waiting for irrigation water which will be supplied by the Black Canyon reclamation project administered by the US Department of the Interior Bureau of Reclamation." Original caption from print. Courtesy of the Library of Congress.

to find a meaningful way to work within the structure. Artists such as Dorothea Lange and Walker Evans often ignored Stryker's specific, scripted demands and pursued their own personal and aesthetic interests, continuing to send back powerful portraits of America in the heart of the Depression. The FSA is instructive as a model because of its large scale and its attempt to be comprehensive. The project amassed more than 250,000 negatives of which approximately 172,000 have been printed and catalogued at the Library of Congress. The work is maintained as a unique collection within the Library of Congress, accessible to any interested researcher, and remains in the public domain without copyright restrictions. This archive will continue to serve as important data for many disciplines as researchers bring new meaning and interpretations to this period in American history through reconsiderations of the photographic information.

In 1965 the National Endowment for the Arts was established, and the first grants in a Photography Surveys category were awarded in 1976. Aimed at promoting artists' descriptions and interpretations of the history and contemporary culture of various regions in the United States, the category supported many regional photographic surveys. Although the FSA served as a model for early discussions about the survey category, the goal was to decentralize the effort, allowing work from the artists and the various regions to determine the scope, scale, and character of each project. Emerging local artists were often brought together with well-known national artists to create a portrait of a town or region. Between forty and fifty surveys were conducted during the six years that the Photographic Surveys category was funded. The importance of these various surveys lies in the efforts to provide a regional base for each project and to support the creative vision and unique perspective of the participating photographers. Valuable debates about the role of the photograph as document, how much to direct photographers in their work, and whether a survey needed to cover specific topics such as architecture, people, and points of interest were central to almost every survey project. Except in a few circumstances, however, there was little collaboration among the photographers on each survey or between the photographers and the residents of the region. While much significant work was generated, there was little oversight and no coherent vision of the context of the work and the role it would play in future histories. The work also had limited public exposure, as many of the photographs were only exhibited in museums or artists' spaces and rarely reached beyond these institutions' audiences into the community. No central catalogue of the photographs was produced during this period, and today, the work remains scattered in local and regional museums and archives around the country.

One of the regional surveys that received generous NEA support was the Rephotographic Survey Project (RSP),[7] conceived and conducted by Mark Klett, JoAnn Verburg, and myself. Many of the ideas and issues for the Water in the West Project can be traced to the concept and structure of the RSP. For three summers the project traveled throughout the West locating more than two hundred sites of nineteenth-century survey photographs made by Jackson, Hillers, Bell, Russell, and O'Sullivan. Modern, comparative views were made from the same camera location, at the same time of day and approximate time of year. Mark Klett, who served as chief photographer for the project, directed a team of artists to conduct the fieldwork and developed a precise methodology for locating and making the comparative images. In addition to the profound geographic, geological, and vegetational changes documented, the project sought to learn more about the context and cultural conditions from which the nineteenth-century photographers worked. Through precise fieldwork, research of primary source materials such as diaries, journals, USGS maps, and survey annual reports, and extensive consultations with experts in the field of American history, landscape architecture and planning, botany, natural history, geology, art history, and environmental studies, the project was able to develop a framework and methodology for working that would allow the photographs to have value beyond their function as art objects.

Several aspects of the Rephotographic Survey directly influenced the Water in the West Project: the collaborative manner of the participants in setting goals and determining structure; the willingness to let the work (the collection of visual information) define the project and its final form, rather than having preconceived notions about what the project would reveal; the role of the artist as "documentarien" and interpreter of historical and contemporary landscape issues; and the interest in producing work that would be meaningful to scholars from many disciplines, both now and in the future.

A major influence on the Water in the West Project has also been the commitment of many of the members to local and regional issues. Mark Klett and I conducted several local history projects in Colorado and Idaho between 1978 and 1981. We worked with such diverse groups as local historical societies, senior citizen centers, and public relations officials for ski resorts. We also collaborated with a Shoshone-Paiute Indian Reservation in southern Idaho to collect historical photographs, conduct oral history interviews, and assist with a traveling exhibition and publication.[8] Peter Goin initiated a landscape survey along the entire length of the U.S.-Mexico border from the Gulf of Mexico to the Pacific Ocean, resulting in the publication of *Tracing the Line*.[9] He also directed the Lake Tahoe Rephotographic Survey, an investigation of how landscape and nature have become managed by human action in the Lake Tahoe, Donner Lake, and Truckee River area.[10] Terry Evans participated in a pilot project for the NEA Photography Survey category in 1974, working with two other photographers to document the landscape, architecture, and people of rural Kansas. The resulting exhibition and catalogue were titled *No Mountains in the Way*.[11] Martin Stupich documented the construction of the Atlanta subway and the rapid urban development of the region under the sponsorship of several NEA-funded survey grants. Robert Dawson worked for several years documenting the effects of large-scale agricultural practices on his birthplace—the Great Central Valley of California.[12] Many of these projects have involved an interdisciplinary approach to reinterpreting history by bringing photographers together with historians, environmentalists, agricultural workers, native Americans, and ranchers. Each of these artists—now members of the Water in the West Project—have produced and assimilated a wide variety of information that contributes to the value of the photograph as an educational tool. These individually sponsored surveys and projects provide primary evidence of the growing need to reinterpret the western landscape. And finally, by testing a variety of theoretical ideas about visual representation, collaboration, and publication, these artists generated the seeds for the founding of the Water in the West Project.

The Water in the West Project has its roots in many of these earlier efforts and specifically came about from Robert Dawson's desire to expand and further enhance his own "Water in the West Project" by including other photographers, historians, and writers, many of whom had significantly influenced the development of his photography. After several years of discussions with Peter Goin, Mark Klett, and myself, an informal planning meeting was scheduled in conjunction with a photography conference "The Political Landscape" in Aspen, Colorado, in 1989. The Aspen conference brought photographers together with western historians, environmental writers, and filmmakers to discuss common concerns about the state of the landscape and environment of the American

West. The first official meeting of the Water in the West Project took place in March 1990 when we gathered several of the photographers from the Aspen meeting together with other interested artists at the Headlands Center for the Arts in Sausalito, California. The Headlands Center was selected as the organizational sponsor for the project because of its innovative programming in literature, visual arts, and performance that deals specifically with cultural history, spirit of place, and social/political/environmental issues. Founding members at this meeting included Laurie Brown, Gregory Conniff, Robert Dawson, Terry Evans, Peter Goin, Wanda Hammerbeck, Mark Klett, Martin Stupich, and myself. Many members had already been interpreting and documenting water issues on some level and were anxious to participate in a collaborative project that might challenge their own way of working as well as provide a broader context for their photography.

At the first meeting, discussions centered around the need to identify exactly what the primary issues were and how this project might address them in a unique and meaningful way. The group agreed that addressing water issues in the American West went beyond merely documenting examples of water use and abuse to include considerations of the relationship of history and culture to nature, landscape, and the environment. The photography of many project members had been influenced by the work of cultural geographer J. B. Jackson, writers Barry Lopez and John McPhee, western historian and novelist Wallace Stegner, sustainable agriculture specialist Wes Jackson, and environmental scholars such as Donald Worster and Marc Reisner. Members were interested in combining these broader issues of cultural history with specific environmental, political, and aesthetic concerns. Discussions followed on the structure and goals of the project, the effectiveness of the collaborative process, the political direction of the work, the audience and how they would be served, how the work would be useful, what other disciplines would be actively involved, what the models were for interdisciplinary collaborations, what the proper context would be for the work, how the photographs might evaluate and add to our understanding of contemporary attitudes toward landscape, and how the project could serve as a model for other interdisciplinary investigations of critical social and environmental issues. The group also stressed the importance of establishing a model of working that placed emphasis on *process* rather than on *product,* for example focusing on the generation of meaningful work for an archive rather than on a final large-scale exhibition or publication. An integral part of this emphasis on process would mean periodically putting their work before the public in the form of small exhibitions, public meetings, and occasional publications in order to promote discourse between the artist and the community.

The project invited a number of specialists from other disciplines to serve as advisors: landscape historian Kenneth Helphand, environmental/water historian Donald Worster, founder of the Land Institute Wes Jackson, artist and administrator Jock Reynolds, arts administrator and public arts specialist Jennifer Dowley, and political economist Michael Black. These individuals asked important questions about the photograph's role as a record of cultural attitudes, how photography can function as a tool for social and political change, and how artists might provide new and unique perspectives on critical environmental issues. It is unusual for artists and scholars to spend such extended periods of time together sharing their knowledge about water issues, landscape history, and the role of the artist in contemporary culture. This process of debate has both informed and enhanced the development of the Water in the West Project and the work of the individual photographers. The project anticipates that these and other advisors will eventually work on selected collaborative projects with photographers from the group.

In order to function effectively, the members agreed to follow a loose democratic structure. The co-directors, Robert Dawson and myself, act as coordinators with most policy decisions being made by the unanimous consent of the members. Each member has agreed to take on certain administrative or organizational responsibilities, encouraging a sense of ownership and accountability for the direction and purpose of the project. Maintaining a spirit of collaboration both in the administration of the project and the production of work was of vital importance to several members of the project. Robert Dawson, Mark Klett, and I brought several years of experience to the project from previous group efforts. As Klett states: "I am interested in the project as an experiment in collaboration—a collaboration among photographers who are committed to western water issues. There may in fact be diverse forms and levels of collaboration which occur between individuals and the group at large. But in general, what I am advocating is a willingness by the participants to place the goals of the group above individual gain. . . . I think this is an extraordinary prospect. . . . And it is different, I think, than our normal routine as photographers where we tend to function self-sufficiently, and at times, even compete with each other." These collaborations could take the form of two members working together on a specific issue, or a photographer working with a western fiction writer or water specialist in a particular region, or a curator/historian working with a photographer to create a museum installation of historical and contemporary photographs. Through this process, project members will be able to learn from the diverse perspectives of other photographers and scholars and will be able to share their creative ways of addressing an issue. The group agreed that the emphasis on collaboration did not preclude members of the project continuing to work on individual projects. Despite the difficulties inherent in collaborative efforts, the group made a strong commitment to the process which they felt provided for a more diverse perspective and tended to keep the issues from becoming entrenched or codified into a single voice.

As the project progressed, several members, in particular Robert Dawson, Peter Goin, and I, felt that there needed to be a stronger political and environmental focus to the work. A significant amount of our time was devoted to discussing the relationship of the photograph as a creative object to the photograph as a tool for political change. Robert Dawson, drawing on his experience of photographing the destruction of Mono Lake and the effects of large-scale corporate farming on the Central Valley of California, expressed his strong belief in the value of the project utilizing the photographic image to shape public opinion. Peter Goin stated, "I have never subscribed to the notion that political content (by definition) trivializes the photographic image. . . . Although I value aesthetic innovation, it should serve the content. Photography is a dramatic and nearly universal means of communication, and has the potential to influence public opinion and policy." He further suggested that the project might actually have a manifesto or statement of purpose which would outline the political direction of the work. Others felt that we needed to embrace a broader range of opinions and not be confined to a single voice on water and landscape issues. Mark Klett responded, "I am uneasy with a manifesto which is exclusively political in nature. For one thing, the term 'political' has been used very broadly of late, and I think we each need to be specific about its applications. And while I am persuaded that issues of advocacy politics have become a focus for critical expression in our time, I can't help feeling that they are not the only goals this group should identify. For example, can we even deal with such a topic without succumbing to latent romanticism or becoming cynics of cultural abuse?

What is it about our experience of water and place that makes this region (and its politics) such a compelling topic for us, so much so that we care about it with great passion?" Terry Evans asked how we as photographers can become advocates for change by speaking the truth about what we see. She further related: "I am not a lobbyist. I am an artist-photographer who is passionately committed to social and environmental issues." Gregory Conniff added: "I am not a politician, but I do have a point of view about water in America. It has been my assumption that this project exists in the first place only because the people involved think something is seriously wrong with the way our society is dealing with water, in arid places especially. My interest in being involved with the project grows from a desire to have a hand in working for change in how we think about water in our lives." He further stated that a primary requirement for the work should be that the images be "useful"—useful to a wide range of disciplines from grassroots political advocates to cultural geographers. He added, "We can do this [be useful] aggressively and semi-passively. Aggressively by means of exhibitions and publications under our design and control. Semi-passively by placing ourselves and our work at the service of others who are pursuing specific goals and could use our skills." Goin finally suggested that we draw up a preamble that "would challenge the group to a course of action and would respect the individual differences and incorporate the rich diversity of ideas within the project."

The group finally arrived at a consensus for a statement of purpose or "preamble" that encompassed a broader perspective and allowed for growth in a variety of directions. The statement is intended as a point of departure—a working document—that will reflect the evolution of the project and the changes it will undergo over time.

> The Water in the West Project is a collaboration of a group of photographers whose art shares strong ties to the landscape of the western United States.
>
> The Project's primary goal is to create a body of work which will contribute to the increasingly urgent dialogue about the future and quality of life on earth as sustained by increasingly limited natural resources.
>
> As a collaborative project, Water in the West represents a wide range of interests and concerns from

agricultural practices in western Kansas to water rights on the Paiute Reservation at Pyramid Lake in Nevada. At the core of the project is a concern for how water use and perceived needs have shaped our natural and social landscape.

Water in the West intends to serve as a clearinghouse for ideas and as a structure to encourage collaborative and interdisciplinary work through the establishment of a comprehensive photographic archive, public lectures and symposia, and a continuing series of publications and exhibitions. The project is seeking writers, historians, visual artists, water specialists, politicians and landscape planners who are interested in participating in the work.

It is important to note that the group supported individuals within the project who wanted to take a more political stance and encouraged their seeking affiliations with local and regional institutions and environmental groups to strengthen the effectiveness of their work. After a year, however, the group was still struggling with the issues of collaboration and direction for the project. Some collaborative efforts had begun but they progressed at a difficult and time-consuming pace. Confronting the fact that a single collaboration involving every member would be extremely difficult, and that the work of the founding members could not adequately represent the range of water issues, Goin and Dawson proposed that the emphasis shift away from the exclusiveness of this core group toward a focus on the development of a more comprehensive archive. After some initial discussion at the Reno meeting their proposal was unanimously accepted. The archive would embrace the spirit of process by becoming the repository of work-in-progress from project members as well as from other interested photographers and scholars throughout the country.

One of the archive's goals is to serve as a major resource of visual arts and related materials on water in the American West. It will include historical photographs of federal, state, and local water projects; vernacular imagery such as snapshots, family albums, and postcards; advertising and travel brochures which use water to promote recreation, housing development, or products; selected reference articles and bibliographies; and contemporary photographs and biographical information on participating artists. The historical imagery in the archive will include photocopies of nineteenth-century government survey work by Timothy O'Sullivan, William Henry

Jackson, John K. Hillers, William Bell, and E. O. Beaman as well as photographs by other established artists of the day such as Eadweard Muybridge, Carleton Watkins, and Andrew J. Russell. Work will be collected from government archives such as the Farm Security Administration, the Historic American Building Survey, other Library of Congress holdings, the Army Corps of Engineers, the Los Angeles Department of Water and Power, and other federal, state, and regional water projects. Research will also concentrate on photographs from personal collections, small regional libraries and historical societies, private and community archives on Indian reservations, and senior citizen groups in an effort to explore the personal, human-interest aspect of this history. In addition, copies of articles and reproductions collected from historical magazines, newspapers, and journals will begin to place the history of attitudes toward water use in a social, cultural, and political context. Historical images from nationally recognized artists such as Ansel Adams, Edward Weston, Laura Gilpin, Russell Lee, Dorothea Lange, and Margaret Bourke-White will be collected from art museums and private collections in the form of reference slides or photocopies. Magazine articles, photographic essays, and books by Eliot Porter, Philip Hyde, and other photographers who contributed to the political efforts of groups such as the Sierra Club, Friends of the Earth, and the Wilderness Society will also become part of the research archive. Historical advertising, travel brochures, posters, albums, postcards, and souvenirs that promoted recreation, urban development, and the western experience will also help the project and future researchers place water issues in a broad social and cultural context. Efforts have already been made to include visual materials in the archive relating to the multicultural history of water in the West, for example the historic Indian water rights controversy at Pyramid Lake, Nevada; Chinese labor in mining towns in the Sierra Nevada and Idaho; water allocation systems and gardening in Japanese internment camps; community-managed Hispanic water systems in New Mexico; Papago farming and ranching in Arizona; Hispanic migrant labor in California agriculture; and small-scale, organic, sustainable farming practiced by various groups throughout the West. The work of contemporary photographers will be represented by reference prints and slides as well as by original, museum-quality exhibition photographs. This collection will include current and previous work by the founding members, archive members, and other photographers doing significant work on water issues.

A major component of the archive will be its focus on including archive members' work. These members

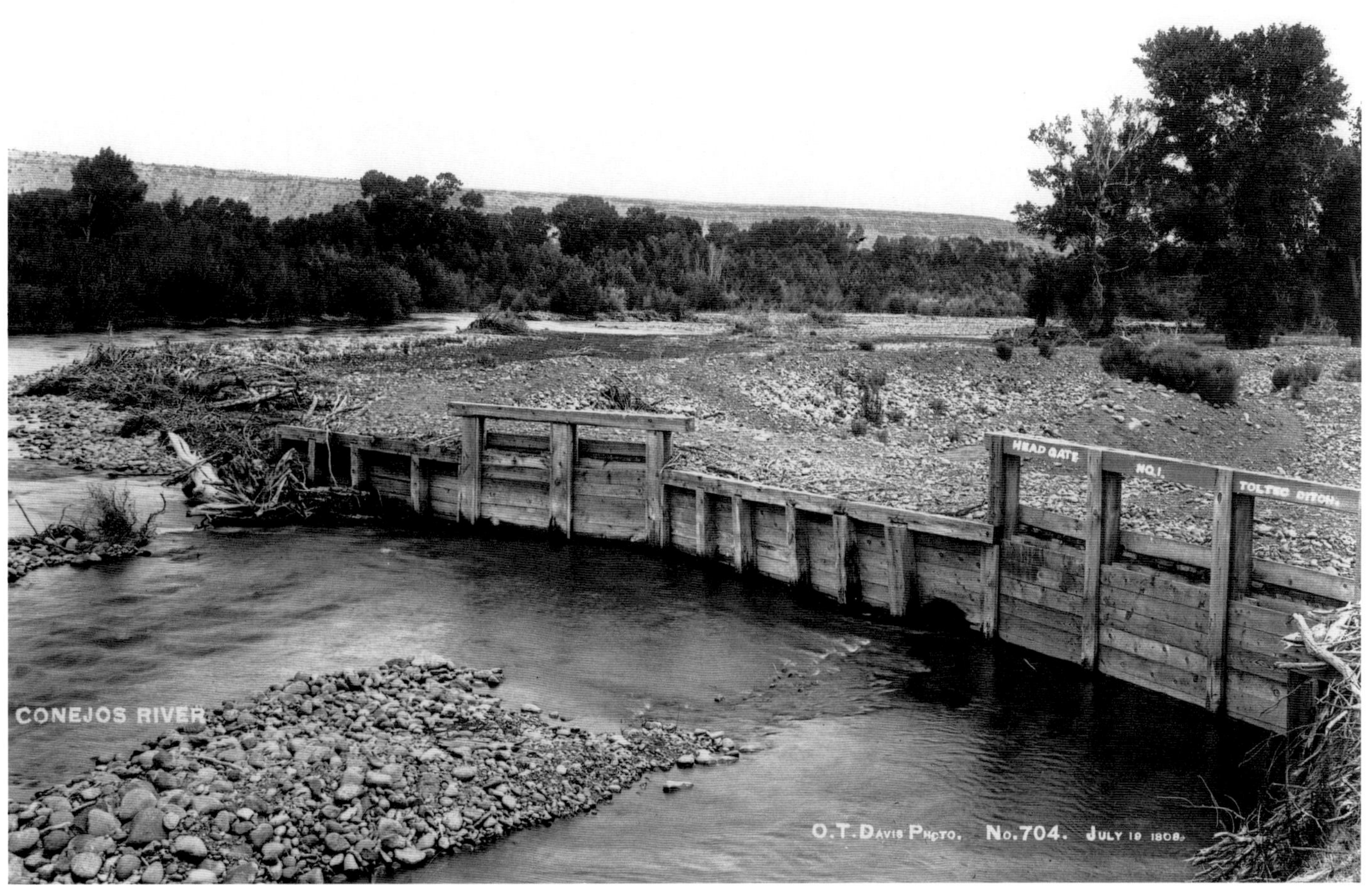

O. T. DAVIS

7. Head Gate No. 1, Toltec Ditch, July 19, 1908. Handmade irrigation gate on the Conejos River, Colorado. Courtesy of the Colorado Historical Society.

will be photographers whose work contributes additional information about topics, regions, or points of view not covered by the founding group. Archive members will submit proposals for projects, which, if accepted, will become a part of the project's archive. From time to time, photographers and writers will be commissioned to work on specific topics or regions that have not been covered by the founding group or the archive members. All of these individuals will be critical to the development of the archive, which will serve as a clearinghouse of visual and written information about water issues in the arid West. As with the historical section, the contemporary part of the archive will also look beyond the art world for images from newspapers, magazines, advertising brochures, and scholarly journals in the fields of landscape architecture, geography, geology, environmental studies, and natural history.

Both founding and archive members determine their own topics and areas of interest to work on throughout the year. In order to make the collection a viable research tool, a yearly review system has been established to evaluate what areas or topics need to be covered. Currently members are working in several regions and focusing on a wide range of topics.

Laurie Brown has long been committed to looking at how our culture has dramatically altered the western landscape. Her previous work involved breaking from the traditional photographic format by collaging historic images into her contemporary prints to provide a sense of extended narrative. Her recent work focuses on the encroachment of southern California development on wild lands (see Plates 8–12). For the Water in the West Project she has turned her attention to water parks and to the lakes, reservoirs, and recreation areas that form the end of the Colorado River Aqueduct and the California Aqueduct. Her photographs of Las Vegas developments with simulated "lakefront property" and desert water parks offering a "nature" experience reflect with poignant irony how our culture has promoted water and the wilderness experience as a commodity. Her panorama format underscores her debt to the nineteenth-century "landscape view." She anticipates combining her contemporary images with historical photographs, many which she has already researched from the Keystone-Mast Collection at the California Museum of Photography in Riverside.

Gregory Conniff has focused his work over the past five years on the midwest and western plains regions (see Plates 13–17). Conniff's interest in water issues came long before his participation in the project. His work has dealt with the relationship of agriculture, cattle ranching, recreation, and power to the drought conditions of the northern plains of North and South Dakota through Colorado. He sees his photographs as less of an indictment and more of a sadness for the "blind way in which we deal with our world . . . the photographs are evidence of misplaced human ambition." His work has been strongly influenced by cultural geography and by what photographs teach us about how we organize and perceive space. He continues to work on a large series, "An American Field Guide," his recent book *Common Ground* being the first volume in the series.[13] In that book he writes: "Facts are everywhere. Facts come first. Their usefulness becomes visible as we push them against one another and wonder about the results. As we become more certain about them, some facts become ideas and then tools for people."

Robert Dawson has been photographing water issues in the West since his work in 1979 documenting the spectacular drying up of Mono Lake. His work became increasingly political as he traveled throughout the West recording the effects of large-scale agriculture and the boom-and-bust cycles of the mining industry on towns and entire regions (see Plates 18–22). He photographed multinational agricultural practices and their effect on the land and people of California's Great Central Valley for a survey project of the same name. He is currently working on a statewide California Toxics Project with physician/photographer Lonny Shavelson, as well as on the Pyramid Lake Project with Peter Goin. Recently, Dawson has become interested in documenting small-scale water control structures such as turn-of-the-century wooden flumes, small dams, and hand-built diversion gates. All of these projects have involved collaborative efforts and a multidisciplinary approach to understanding the landscape through oral interviews, historical research, and local and regional exhibitions of the work.

Peter Goin brings to the project a strong commitment to understanding how landscape evolves and is created by culture. For many years, Goin has explored water-related issues in the Great Basin region (see Plates 23–27) and is currently documenting how our culture creates artificial "nature." In addition to directing the Rephotographic Survey of Lake Tahoe and the recent publication of his nuclear landscape work, he continues to photograph evidence of declining water resources. This work includes documenting reservoirs, dry lake beds, and prehistoric lakes. Goin is also working on the Pyramid Lake Project with Robert Dawson, documenting the Truckee River system from its headwaters at Lake Tahoe, through the urban areas of Reno, to its varied outlets at Pyramid Lake, Winnemucca Dry Lake, and Stillwater Wildlife Refuge. The river and the project have become a powerful metaphor for the complex relationships between urban and rural needs, natural vs. managed water systems, agriculture vs. recreation, and farming and ranching vs. native American fishing rights. Goin frequently tries to place his work in a broader cultural context by seeking alternative venues for its publication and exhibition and by working with creative writers, historians, and scientists.

Terry Evans has been documenting the landscape near her home in western Kansas. Her earlier work emphasized such regional issues as preserving endangered prairie grasslands and wetland habitats. Her more recent work documents the mixing of traditional large-scale agriculture with uncultivated lands, native prairie, and areas of sustainable agriculture. Much of her new work is aerial and now includes military and industrial uses of prairie lands (see Plates 28–32). Evans brings to the project a deep personal and spiritual connection to landscape and water issues. Since 1983 she has worked closely with Wes Jackson and the Land Institute to seek meaningful ways for her photographs to complement their efforts to preserve the prairie and promote sustainable agriculture. "Photographing water issues in this region started out as an intellectual idea, but now the work itself is beginning to direct me in intuitive ways. . . . Each place has been exciting and challenging to photograph, each is significant because of drought, irrigation diversion or threatened wildlife habitat. . . . The work has become deeply compelling to me already." She views nature as a "model for making decisions" and sees photographs as agents for significant and meaningful change in our culture. Evans has gone on to work with Greg Conniff photographing farming and cattle ranching along the 98th meridian from the Dakotas to Kansas. In addition she and Conniff have begun working on a project documenting the acequias of northern New Mexico—the centuries-old, community-managed, ditch-irrigation system. They will be investigating the benefits of this small-scale, communal system and looking at the current political conflicts over water rights with outsiders.

Wanda Hammerbeck's interest in land and landscape issues can be traced to her "Depositions" work in 1975 where she utilized archaeological field methodologies and pictographs with text to parody contemporary life and art. Her work progressed to large-scale color landscape work, eventually leading to the combination of photographs and text to "explore our relationship to the land and to the civilization we build out of that relationship" (see Plates 33–37). She states "my need to photograph is much deeper than art-making activity. It keeps me engaged in life and makes meaning for me." In Hammerbeck's most recent work she has turned her camera to her own backyard—the Los Angeles River, tracing its route from the headwaters above Sepulveda Dam, through the movie studios, past Forest Lawn Memorial Park, through the oil-pumping fields, into the industrial bowels of the southland, past the *Queen Mary*, and finally, into the Pacific Ocean at Long Beach. Hammerbeck states "the Los Angeles River provides a metaphor for urban life in the West, for it too has had its fate sealed in concrete. The river runs through land where a total of 84 languages other than English are known by the children of the L.A. school system. People are murdered, bodies dumped along the river like debris, while others fall into its swollen waters during storms and lose their lives. Teenagers spray paint graffiti, some to mark turf, others to decorate and simply make marks. . . . Babies are born along the river, men and women bathe in the river and sleep along its banks. . . . Others romance, ride horses, bicycle and even boat in the concrete channel of the river." Hammerbeck has staked out a difficult subject area which challenges many of our established notions about "the West," about controlling nature to "protect" ourselves, about "life on the river," and about the life-sustaining, spiritually renewing aspects of a river in a community. Her work addresses the contradictions and ironies inherent in the domination and control of a once wild river. For Hammerbeck, the Los Angeles River becomes a symbol for the attitudes our culture has adopted that separates self from nature, and leads to nature's exploitation and abuse. She continues to experiment with various combinations of text and image and with innovative ways of exhibiting her photography. Eventually, she hopes to place her work in a broader context by using historical images from the area showing early flooding, riverbed changes, and the construction of the viaduct.

Mark Klett brings to the project extensive experience with collaborative photographic efforts and a strong body of work from fifteen years of documenting the arid West. His interest in collaborative projects is seen in his participation as chief photographer for the Rephotographic Survey Project, his involvement as an artist on the Central Arizona Project, his work on Headlands Center for the Arts' *Headlands: The Marin Coast at the Golden*

Gate,[14] and his position as director of the Print Collaborative Facility at Arizona State University. For the past nine years Klett has focused his work on the lower Colorado River Basin and, more recently, the San Juan River region (see Plates 38–42). His work reflects interest in tracing the phenomena and experiences that form human interaction with place. "I'm interested in making photographs which comment on the experience of a place as well as describe it. My position has not typically been one of advocacy for or against any political position. But I regard photographs as commentary, and that includes, at times, taking a specific political viewpoint on an issue. I'm interested in how the political struggle for power attempts to effect, or has effected, the kinds of experiences one can have while actually out there. So I tend to view water in our arid region as the focus point, or battleground, for major temporal and physical issues which include the politics of power (and its subcategories such as agricultural vs. urban uses, allocations to states and reservations, recreation, industrialization, etc.). But I also view it as the locus of a cultural history which intertwines the mythic dream of prosperity with the desire for personal redemption." In the future, Klett is planning to document Phoenix's ancient and contemporary canal system and its relationship to the Salt River and to the city of Phoenix. He will work with historical photographs as well as explore evidence of Hohokam use of the ancient canal system to tap the Salt River in order to irrigate crops. Klett is particularly interested in the contemporary uses of the canals for municipal water transport, recreation, public art projects, and riparian habitat.

Martin Stupich has been photographing large-scale engineering works in the western United States since 1980. Prior to joining the Water in the West Project his work concentrated primarily on dams, bridges, irrigation systems, and open-pit mining operations. He has expanded his work to include rivers along the lower Colorado, the Salt and the Gila watersheds in the southwest, and the Columbia River in the northwest. To accentuate the scale of these monuments, much of Stupich's work involves collaging multiple images together to create impressive panoramic views (see Plates 43–47). Stupich writes: "The work I do as a photographer is motivated by a curiosity about the way culture creates landscape. The most prodigious manipulators of the surface of the planet are engineers. Engineers work only as hired hands to realize the aspirations of their clients: in general, us. They design, and cause to rise, structures which western culture calls 'wonders of the world.' Although small engineering is sometimes spectacular (pacemakers and silicon encyclopaedias), my love is for the immensity and audacity that is less subtle and often of more questionable value—those things which transform and compromise the landscape in ways which mortals regard as permanent: dams across canyons, half-mile-deep mines six miles across, canals which separate hemispheres and link oceans. My interest in photographing mammoth cultural artifacts does more than just entertain me. It gives my politic a set of fixed points to steer by: these monuments, as irrefutable evidence of our collective intent, become the focus of my respect, of my awe, my outrage."

As these photographers and new archive members begin to expand their interests, future areas of study for the project might include major drainage/river systems such as the Colorado River basin or the Columbia from headwaters to sea, particular political or geographic boundaries, such as the state of Colorado, the 40th parallel, the 100th meridian, the Canadian and Mexican borders, or a Navajo Reservation, or specific local or regional sites such as urban Los Angeles or the Snake River Valley in Idaho. Also, photographers might contribute work that addresses specific issues such as the role of the military, toxics, mining, energy and power, recreation, agriculture, and urban development in water history. In addition, the archive may include a collection of photographs that incorporate symbolic and metaphorical issues such as the relationship of spirit to place in native American culture.

The archive will be set up to serve not only as a picture agency for magazines, newspapers, journals, and books, but also as a research collection for curators, scholars, writers, and historians. In addition, it will function as an internal vehicle for evaluating the work and ideas of the project on a continuing basis.

This book and the exhibition that it documents are the first in a series of occasional publications, exhibitions, and forums aimed at placing the project's work in a broad, interdisciplinary, and public context. The exhibition at the University of Nevada, Reno, the concurrent humanities' symposium and publication,[15] and this book were conceived as work-in-progress—a laboratory for the collection and assessment of ideas, and as a vehicle for bringing discussions of national and regional water issues to local residents. At the Reno meeting, the project continued to seek important feedback and new ideas from a diverse constituency such as ranchers, writers, developers, historians, policymakers, and water specialists. Among these individuals were environmental historian Donald Worster, American history scholar Donald Pisani, Pyramid Lake Paiute tribal member Joe Ely, and environmental historian Roderick Nash. The exhibition at the Sheppard Fine Art Gallery of the University of Nevada, Reno, included museum-quality photographic prints as well as walls of work prints, contact sheets, and maps from each member of the project. Additional historical photographs documenting the Newlands Irrigation Project (the first federal irrigation project in 1906) were contrasted with publicity stills promoting "water as plenty" from the public relations bureaus of Las Vegas casinos. These photographs, from the university's Special Collections Department, were selected by art students and exhibited in the adjoining SXN gallery. The exhibits and humanities' symposia encouraged meaningful dialogue between project members and the diverse northern Nevada communities whose experiences with water issues were on a very personal, practical, and daily basis. These programs were important in helping writers, historians, and water specialists learn how to read photographs and to reconsider photography's importance in understanding and defining historical and contemporary attitudes toward the land. Donald Worster, for example, in a meeting with the project members after the symposium, commented about how he was reconsidering the value and role of the photograph as a reflection of cultural values and how artist/photographers have made significant contributions to historical information.

The next public meeting and exhibition, modeled on the Reno format, was held at the Land Institute in Salina, Kansas, in October 1991. The group met with founder Wes Jackson and the staff and interns of the institute to discuss how the work might be useful to the study and promotion of sustainable agriculture and the native prairie landscape. An exhibition of work-in-progress and a public discussion at the Salina Art Center furthered the members' commitment to the process of public discourse by taking the project to a variety of communities throughout the West. Future meetings are scheduled at the National Museum of American Art in Washington, D.C., the Desert Studies Center in Zzyzx, California, in the Mojave Desert, and the Los Angeles County Museum of Art.

Clearly this is an ambitious project. Photography is uniquely suited to address the complex history of water in the West in part because its invention and development parallels the history of Anglo-European expansion beyond the 100th meridian. The photograph defined the West with a power and persuasion that is still evident today. Consequently it is only logical that the Water in the West Project members will use their photography to investigate and challenge conventional landscape imagery and the predominant cultural myths and attitudes that have created the irony of the West's arid waters. We don't have the answers, but we hope that this project suggests the beginning of a process to establish a new value system for our relationship to the land.

Ellen Manchester

NOTES

1. Donald Worster, *Rivers of Empire* (New York: Pantheon Books, 1985).
2. Solomon N. Carvalho, *Incidents of Travel and Adventure in the Far West; With Col. Frémont's Last Expedition Across the Rocky Mountains: Including Three Months Residence in Utah, and a Perilous Trip Across the Great American Desert to the Pacific, by S.N. Carvalho, Artist to the Expedition* (New York: Derby & Jackson, 1857).
3. Mark Klett, *Traces of Eden: Travels in the Desert Southwest.* Essay by Denis Johnson, text by Peter Galassi (Boston: David R. Godine, 1986).
4. Peter Goin, *Nuclear Landscapes* (Baltimore: Johns Hopkins University Press, 1991).
5. Robert Dawson, *Robert Dawson Photographs.* Introduction by Ellen Manchester (Tokyo: Gallery Min, 1988).
6. Terry Evans, *Prairie: Images of Ground and Sky.* Introductory essays by Wes Jackson and Gregory Bateson (Lawrence: University Press of Kansas, 1986).
7. Mark Klett, Ellen Manchester, and JoAnn Verburg, *Second View: The Rephotographic Survey Project* (Albuquerque: University of New Mexico Press, 1984).
8. Whitney McKinney, *A History of the Shoshone-Paiutes of the Duck Valley Indian Reservation.* With contributions by E. Richard Hart and Thomas Zeidler (Salt Lake City: Howe Brothers and the Institute of the American West, 1983).
9. Peter Goin, *Tracing the Line: A Photographic Survey of the Mexican-American Border.* Limited edition artist's book, 1987.
10. Peter Goin, *Stopping Time: A Rephotographic Survey of Lake Tahoe* (Albuquerque: University of New Mexico Press, 1992).
11. James Enyeart, *No Mountains in the Way* (Lawrence: University of Kansas Museum of Art, 1975).
12. Gerald Haslam, *The Great Central Valley Project: Photographs by Robert Dawson and Stephen Johnson* (Berkeley: University of California Press, 1992).
13. Gregory Conniff, *Common Ground: An American Field*

Guide (New Haven: Yale University Press, 1985).

14. Paul Metcalf, *Headlands: The Marin Coast at the Golden Gate. A Photographic and Research Collaboration with Miles DeCoster, Mark Klett, Mike Mandel and Larry Sultan* (Albuquerque: University of New Mexico Press and Headlands Center for the Arts, 1989).

15. Joseph Finkhouse and Mark Crawford, eds. *A River Too Far: The Past and Future of the Arid West*. Photographs by the Water in the West Project (Reno: Nevada Humanities Committee and the University of Nevada Press, 1991).

PHOTOGRAPHS

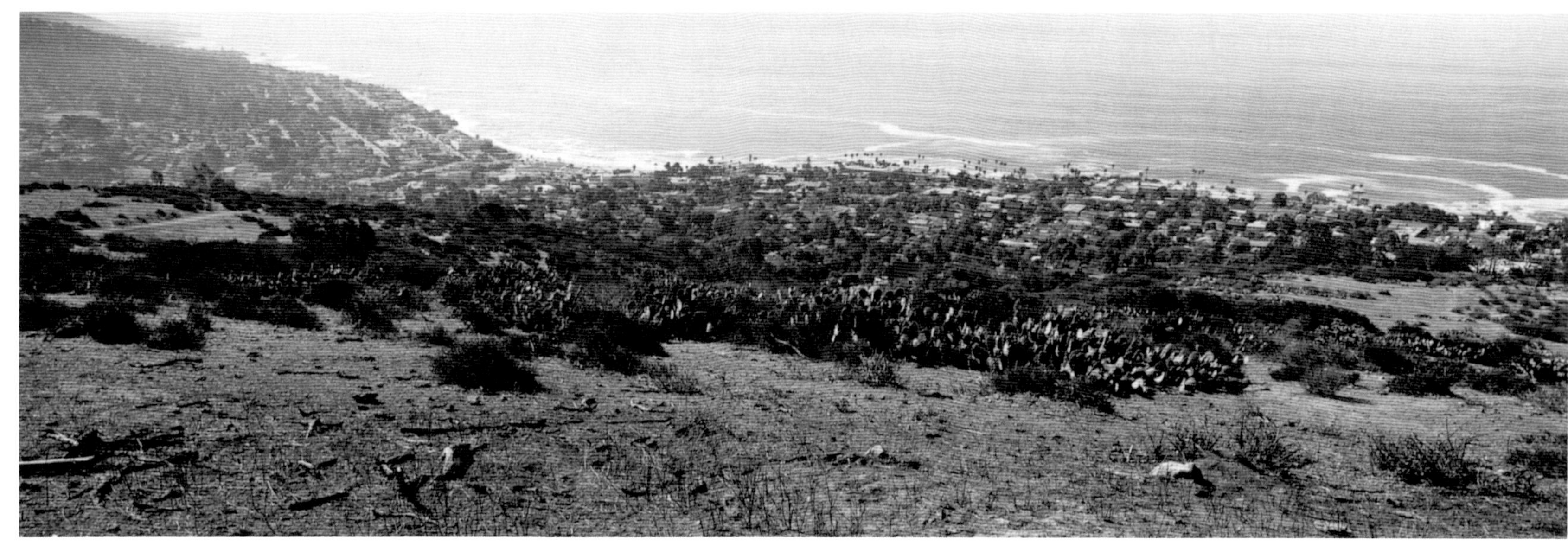

LAURIE BROWN

8 & 9. (diptych) On the Edge, Laguna Beach, California, 1991.

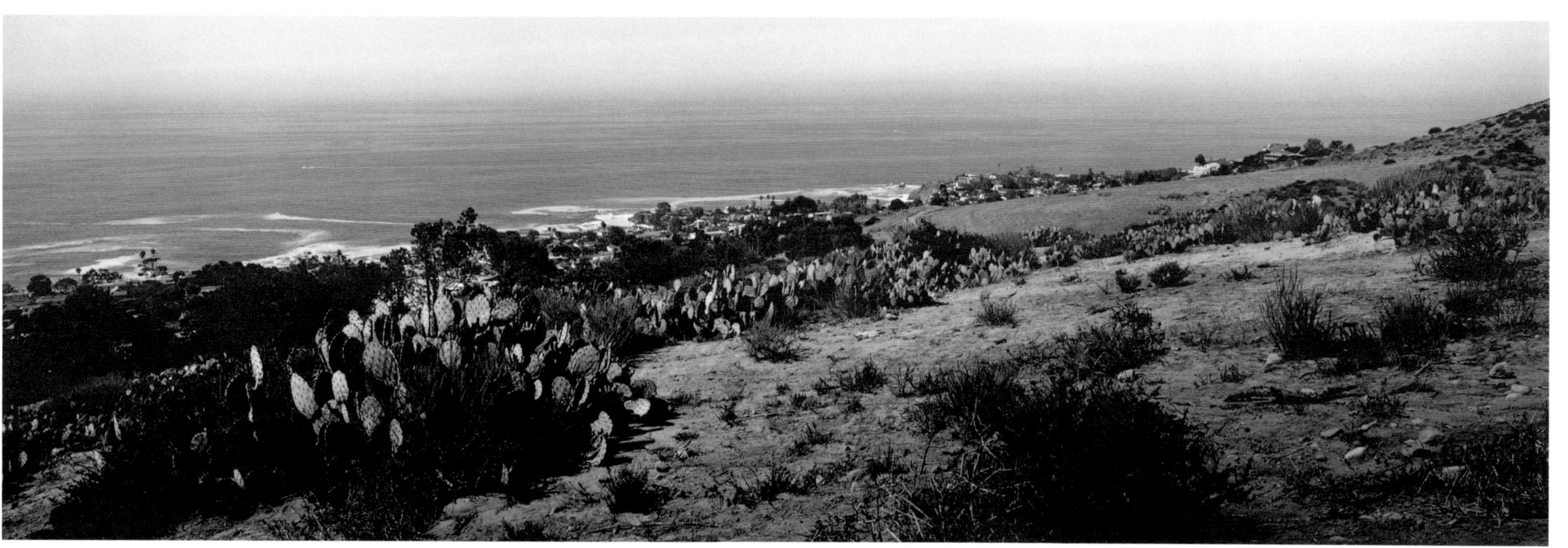

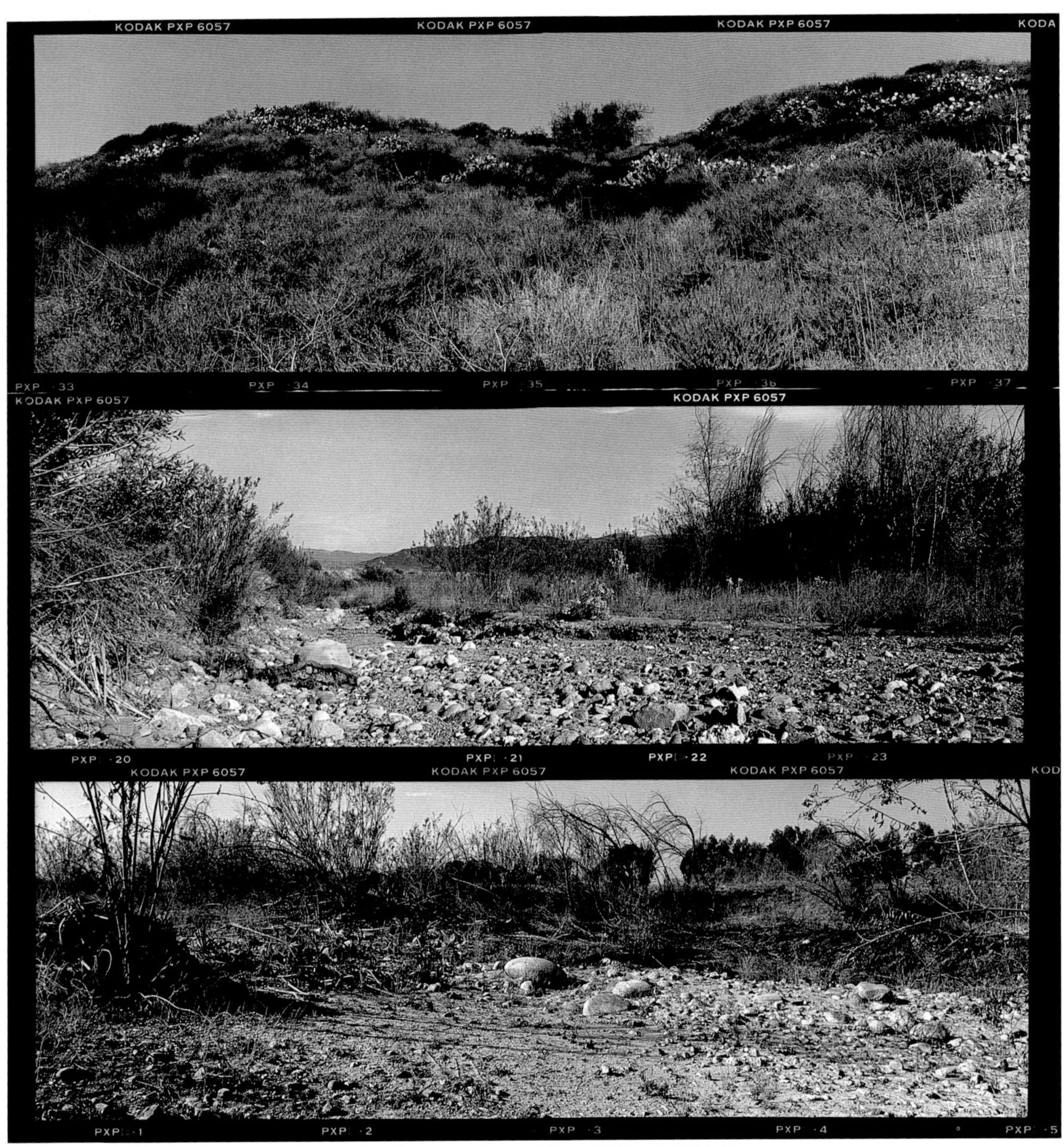

LAURIE BROWN

10. San Juan Capistrano Creek, San Juan Capistrano, California, 1991.

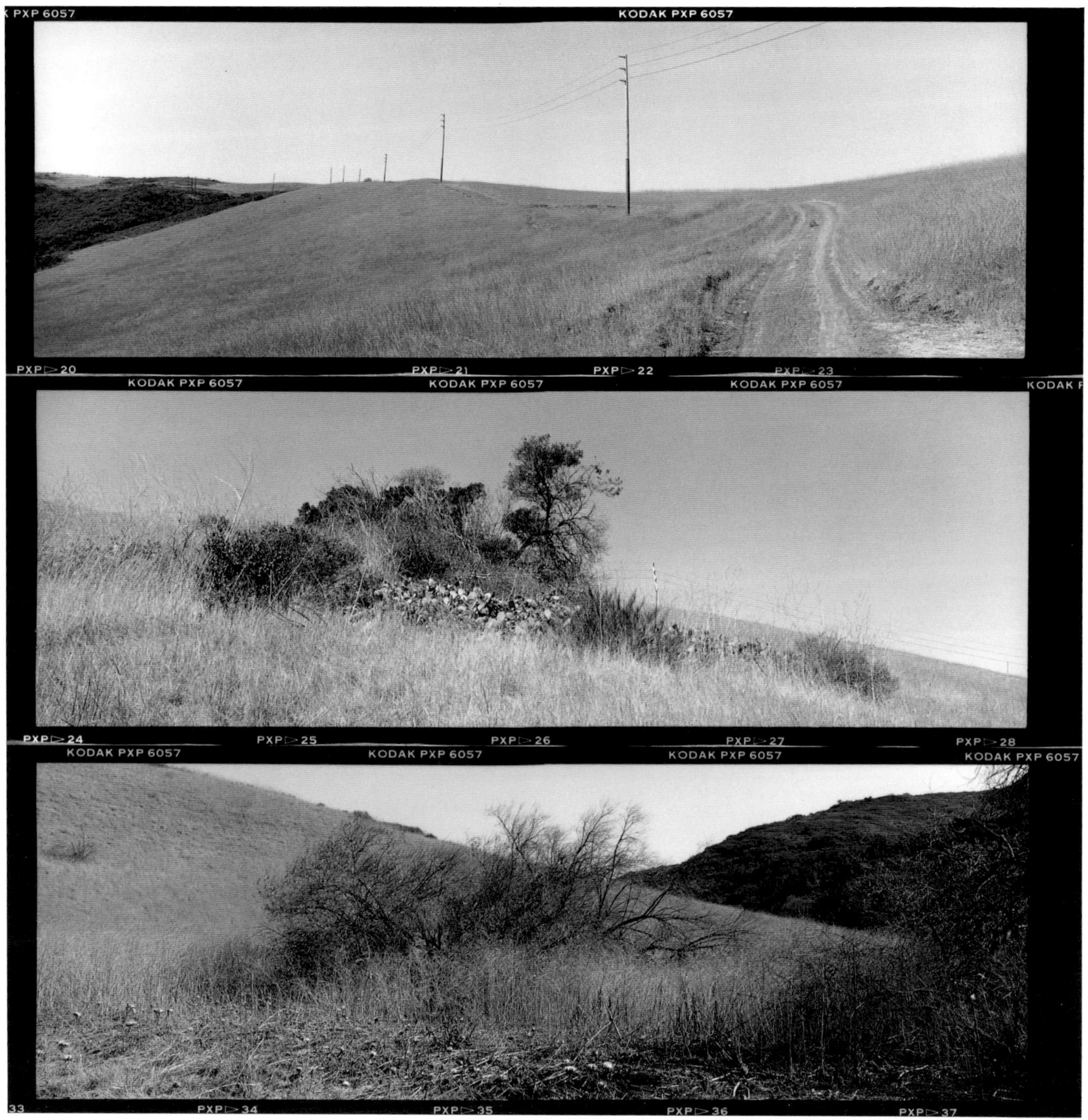

LAURIE BROWN

11. El Morro State Park, Laguna Beach, California, 1991.

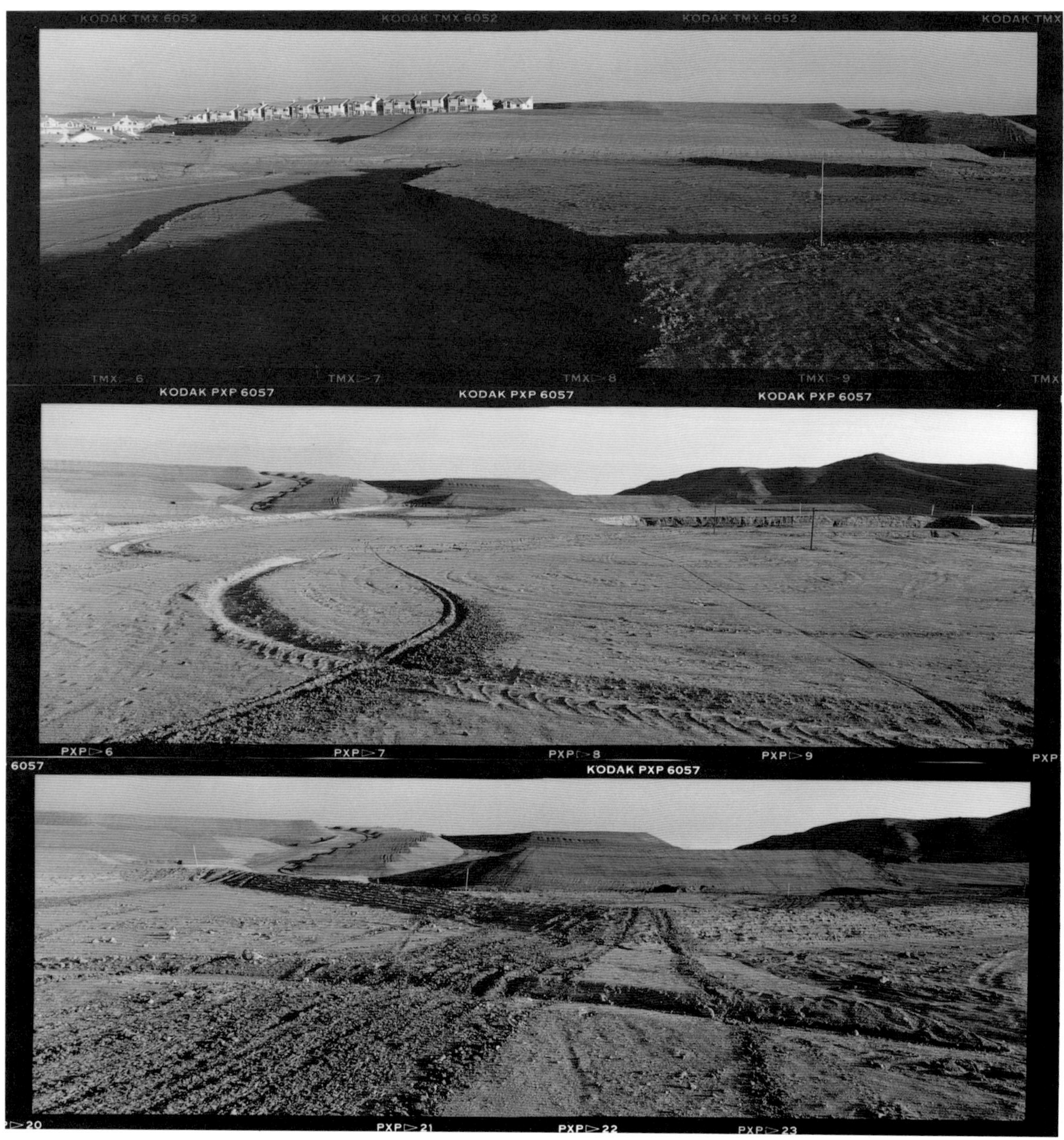

LAURIE BROWN

12. Laguna Hills, California, 1991.

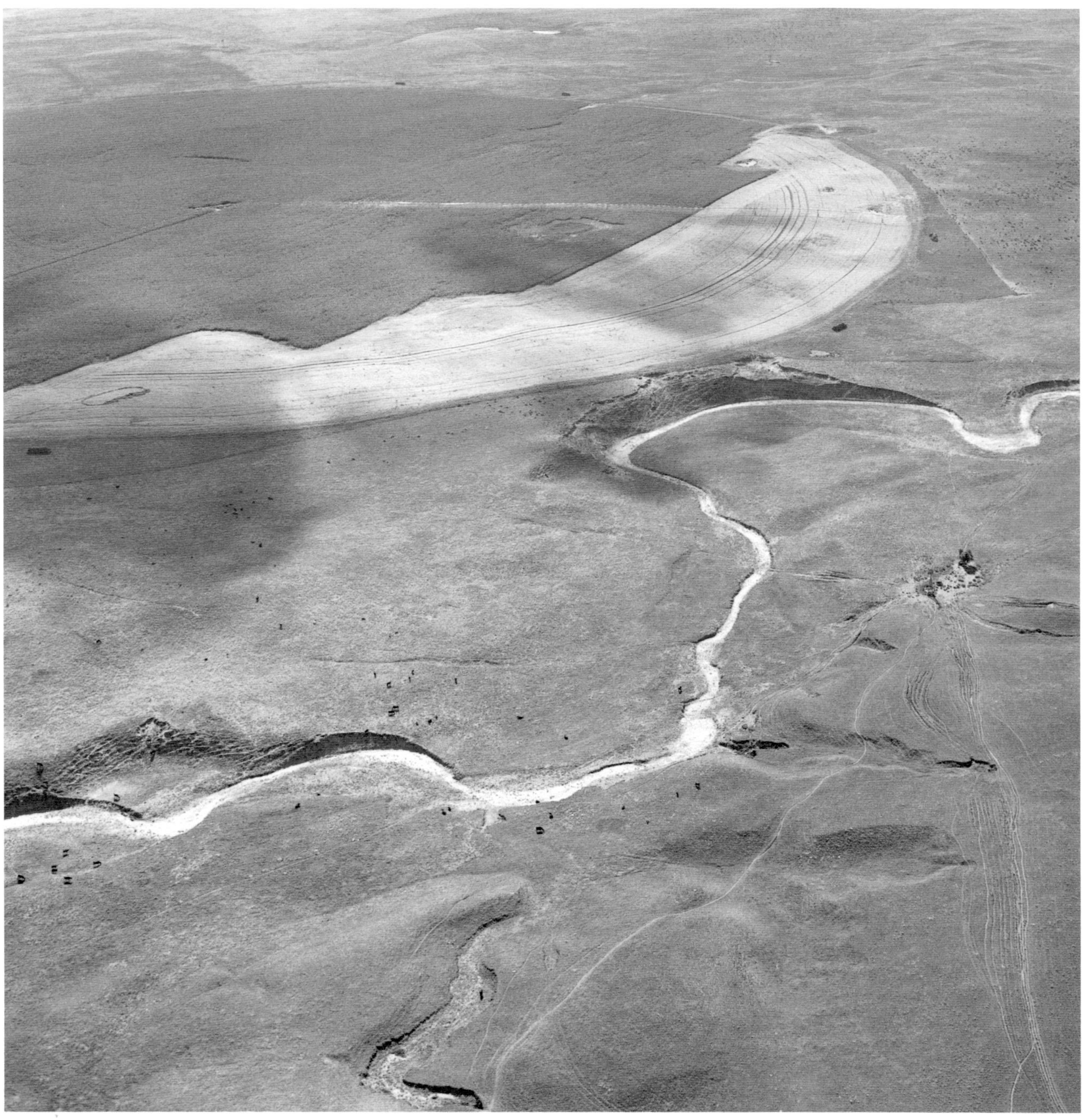

GREGORY CONNIFF

13. Circle Pivot Irrigation, Niobrara River, Stock Tank, Nebraska, 1990.

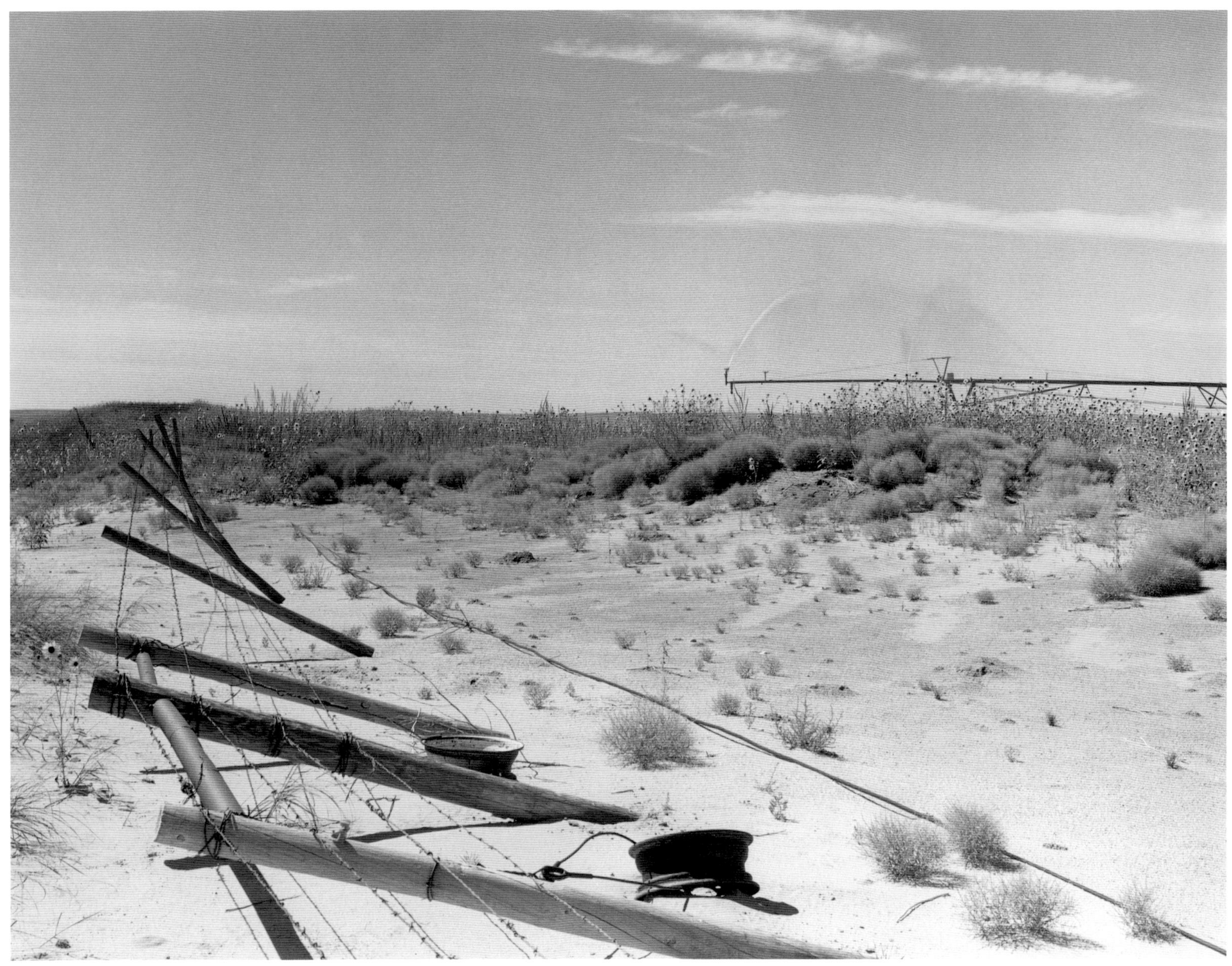

GREGORY CONNIFF

14. Irrigation, near Gordon, Nebraska, 1990.

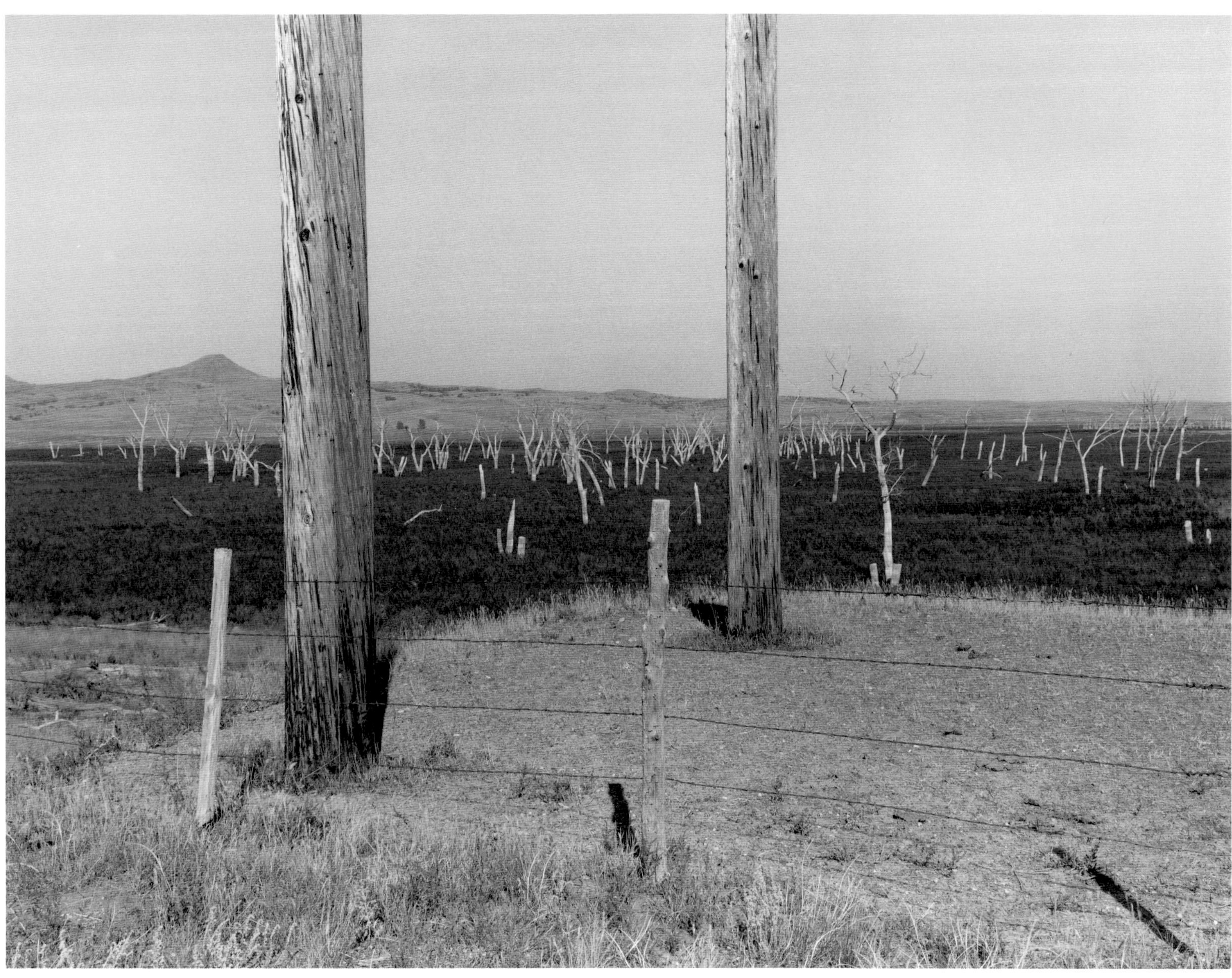

GREGORY CONNIFF

15. Lake Oahe, North Dakota, Dry Backwater, Forest Reemerging in Drought, 1989.

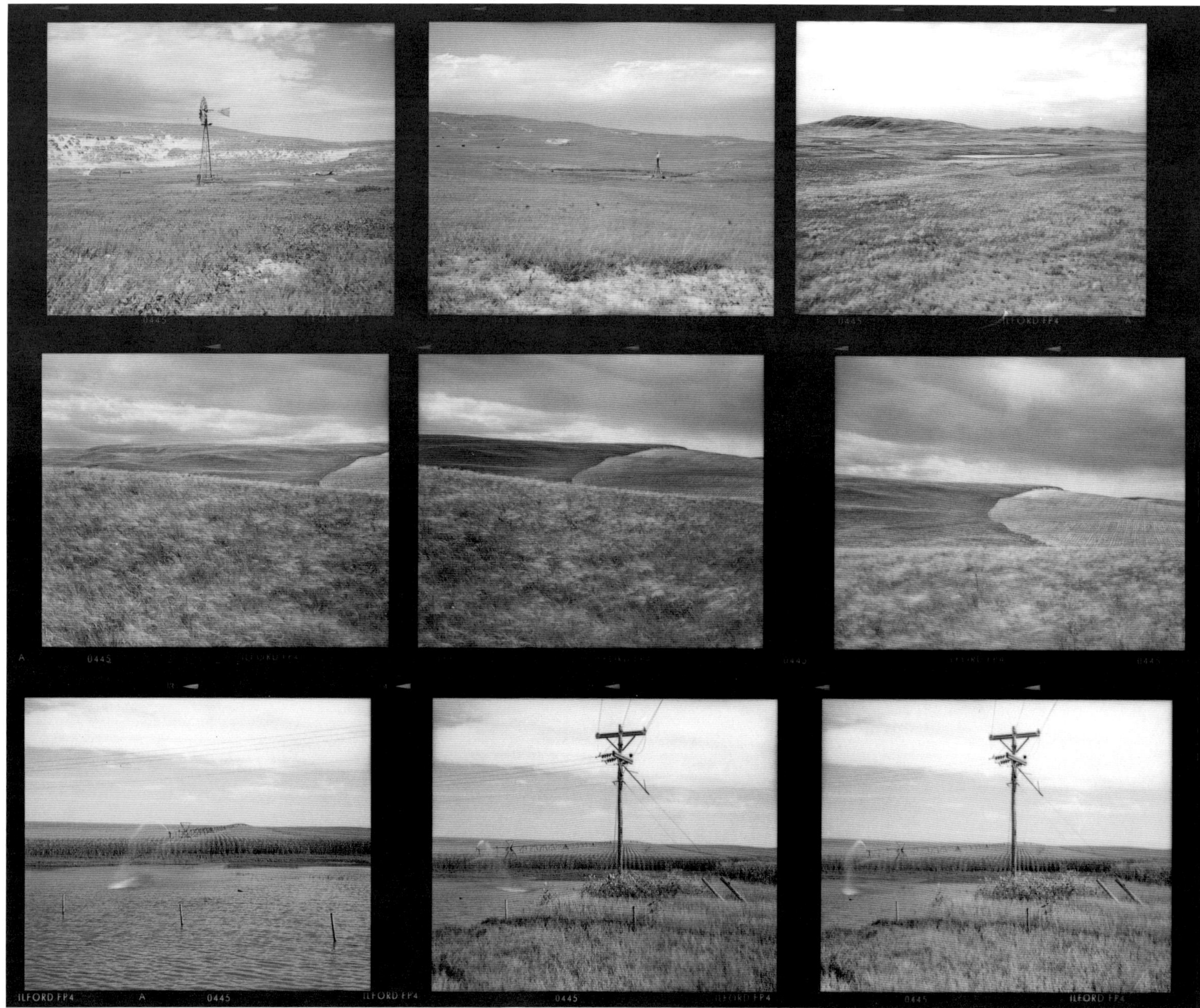

GREGORY CONNIFF

16. Cattle Water and Circle Pivot Irrigation, Sand Hills, Nebraska, 1990.

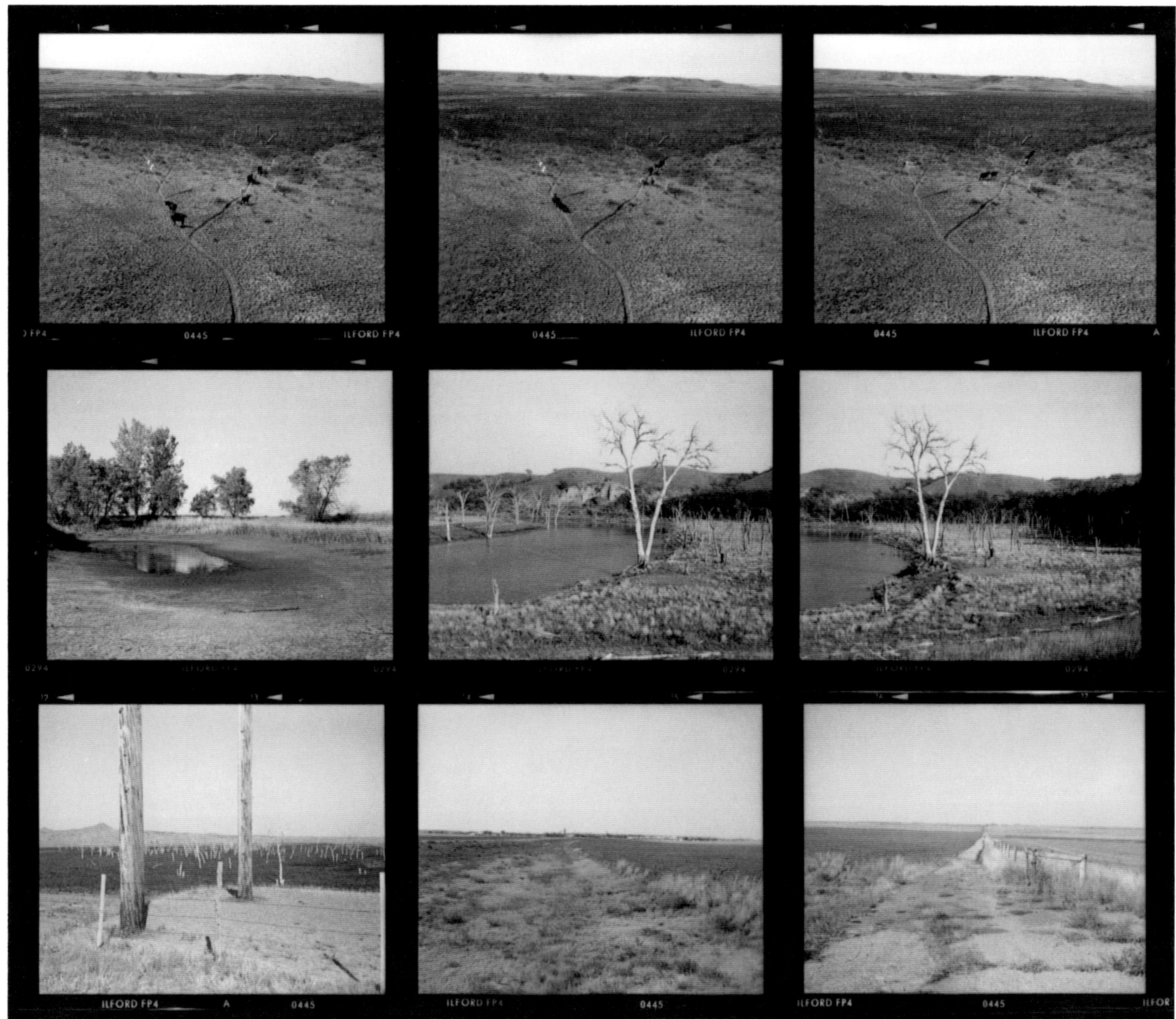

GREGORY CONNIFF

17. Lake Oahe (Impounded Missouri River) in Drought. Cattle Grazing in Bottomland, Drowned Forests Reemerging, 1989.

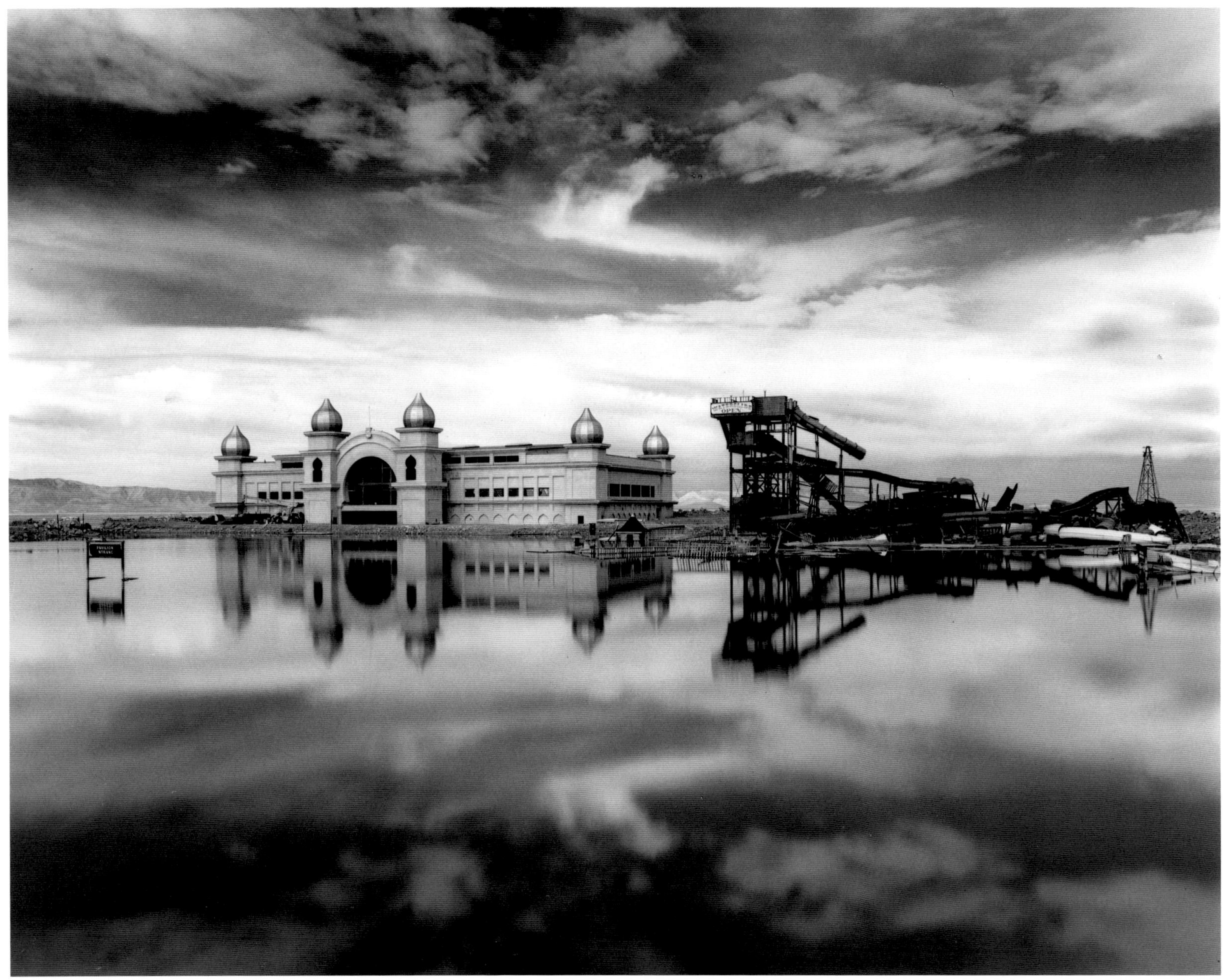

ROBERT DAWSON

18. Flooded Saltair Pavilion, Great Salt Lake, Utah, 1985.

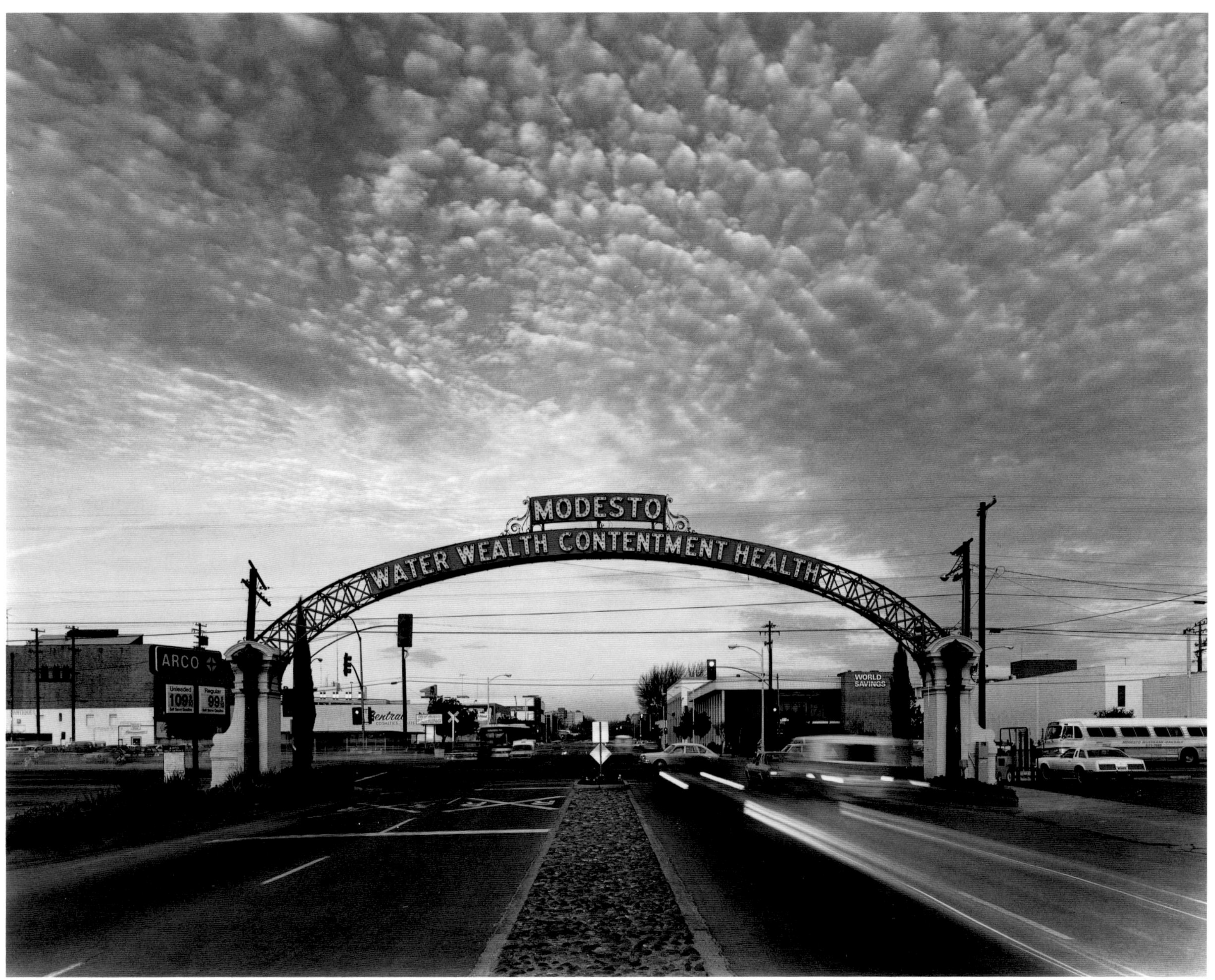

ROBERT DAWSON

19. Modesto Arch, Modesto, California, 1986.

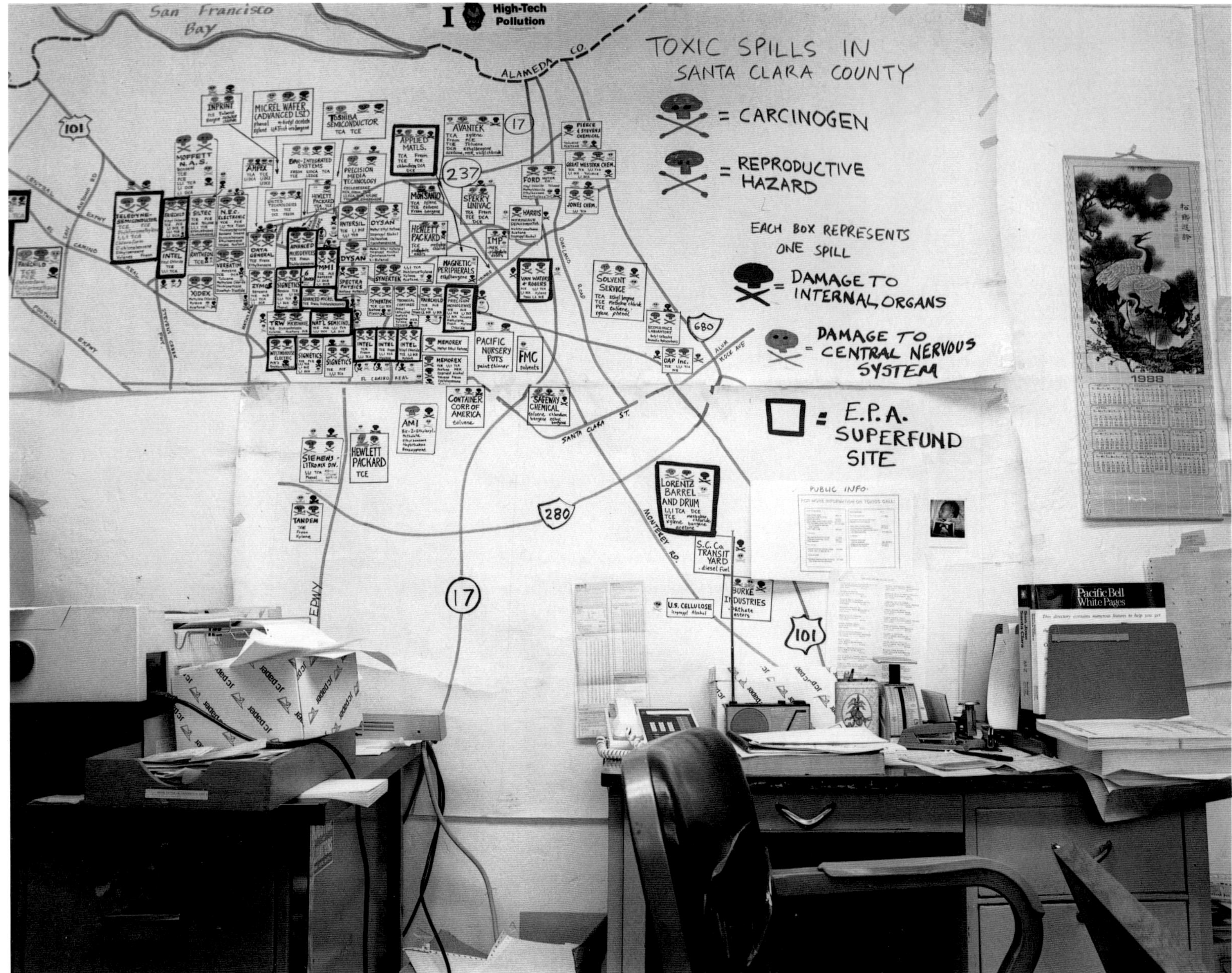

ROBERT DAWSON

20. Map of Toxic Spills, Santa Clara County, San Jose, California, 1989.

This area has the highest concentration of E.P.A. Superfund Cleanup Sites in the nation.

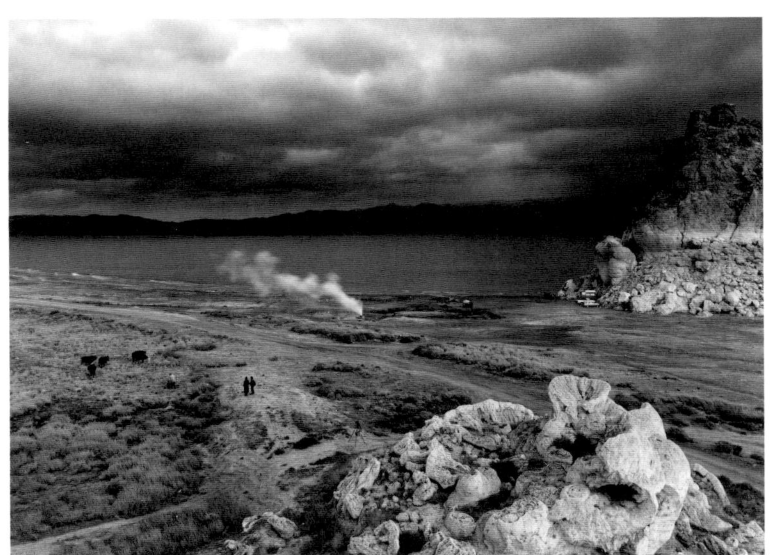
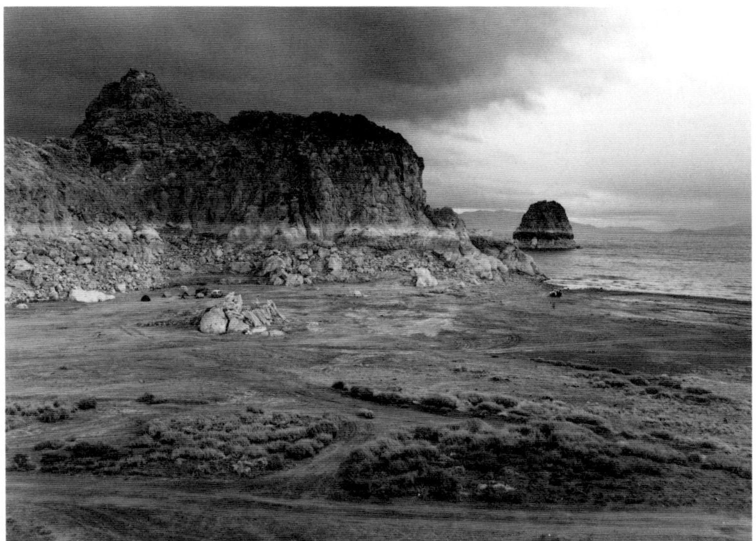

ROBERT DAWSON

21. The Needles, Pyramid Lake, Nevada, 1990. From the Pyramid Lake Project.

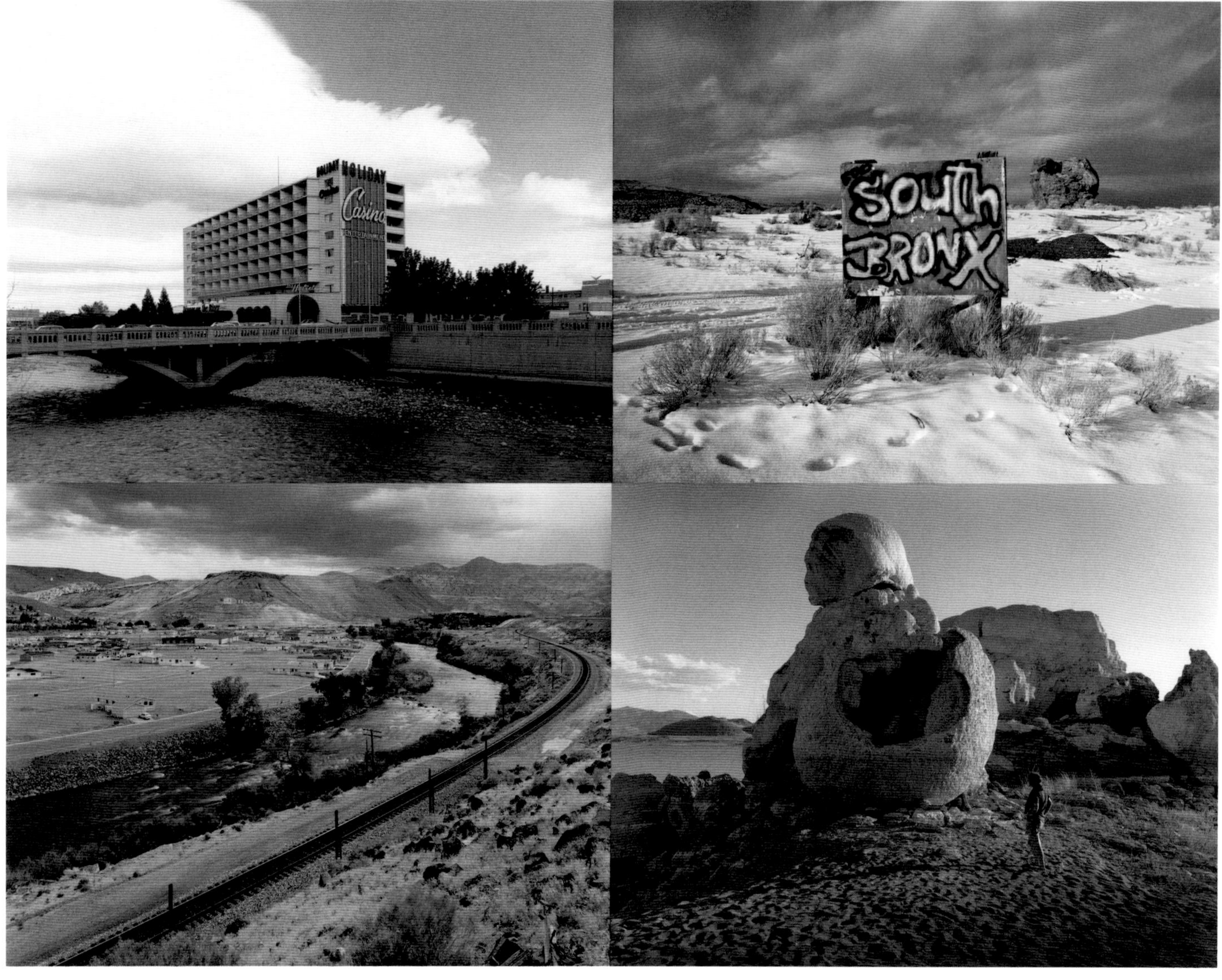

ROBERT DAWSON

22A. Casino, Reno, Nevada, 1990. From the Pyramid Lake Project.

22B. Sign, Paiute Indian Reservation, Pyramid Lake, Nevada, 1989. From the Pyramid Lake Project.

22C. New Homes Built on Flood Plain, Truckee River, Nevada, 1990. From the Pyramid Lake Project.

22D. Stone Mother, Pyramid Lake, Nevada, 1990. From the Pyramid Lake Project.

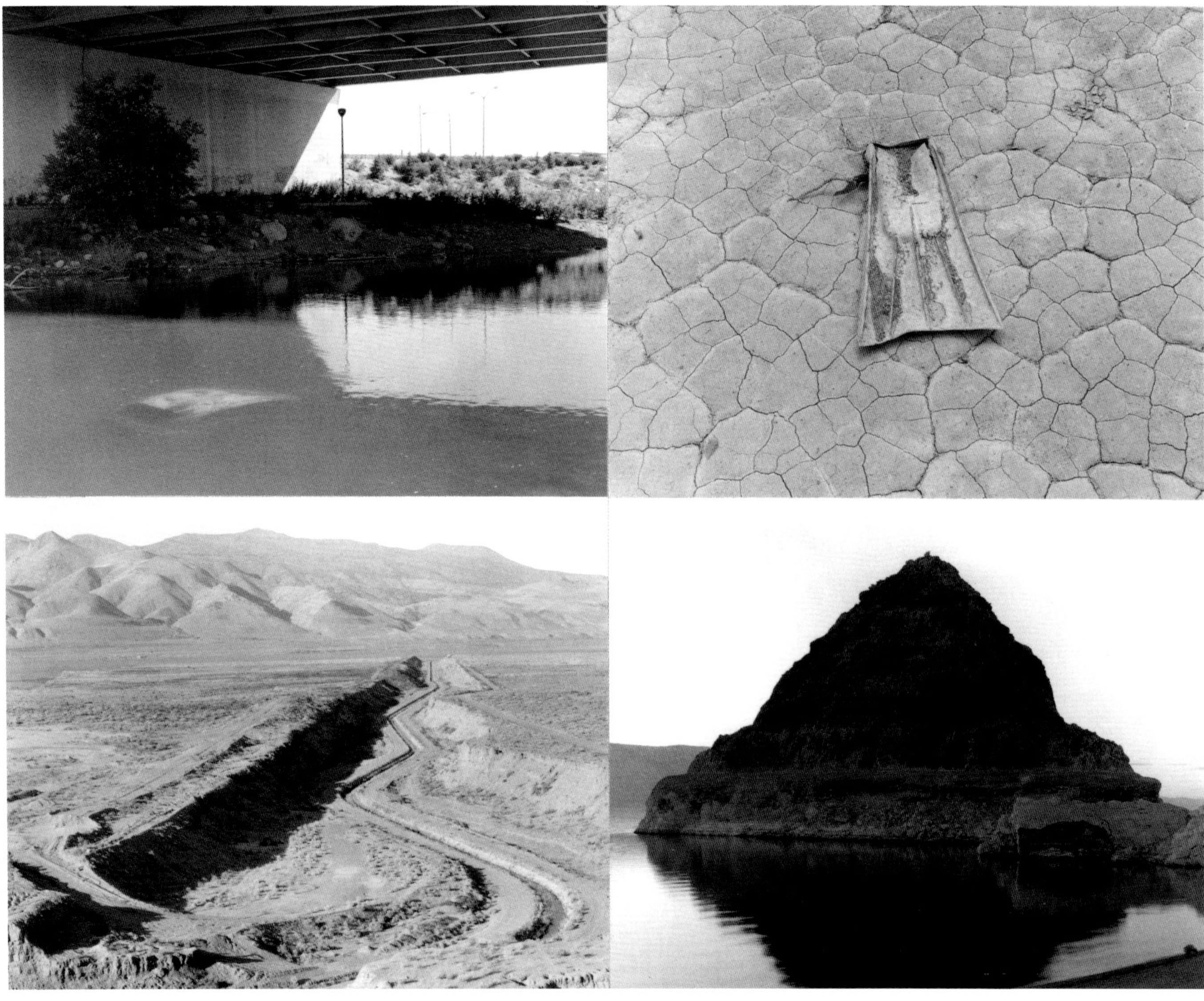

PETER GOIN

23A. Submerged Car in Truckee River, Highway 395 Bridge, Sparks, Nevada, 1990. From the Pyramid Lake Project. (original in color)

23B. Abandoned Swim Fin on Dry Lake Bed near Nixon, Nevada, 1990. From the Pyramid Lake Project. (original in color)

23C. Causeway for Truckee River at Pyramid Lake, Nevada, 1989. From the Pyramid Lake Project. (original in color)

23D. The Pyramid at Dusk, Pyramid Lake, Nevada, 1990. From the Pyramid Lake Project.

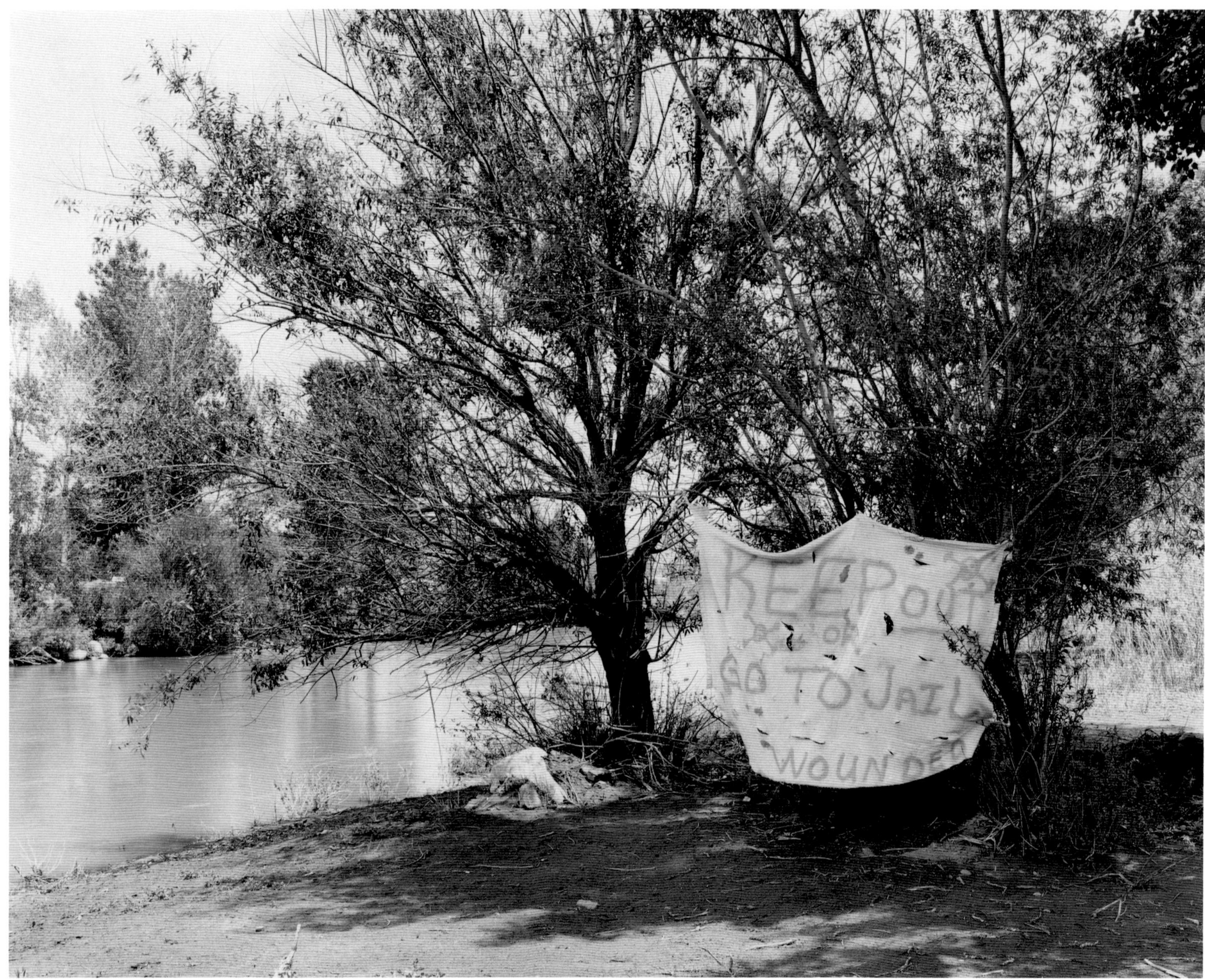

PETER GOIN

24. "Keep Out or Go to Jail Wounded." Makeshift sign along no-man's-land, Truckee River, Sparks, Nevada, 1989.

From the Pyramid Lake Project. (original in color)

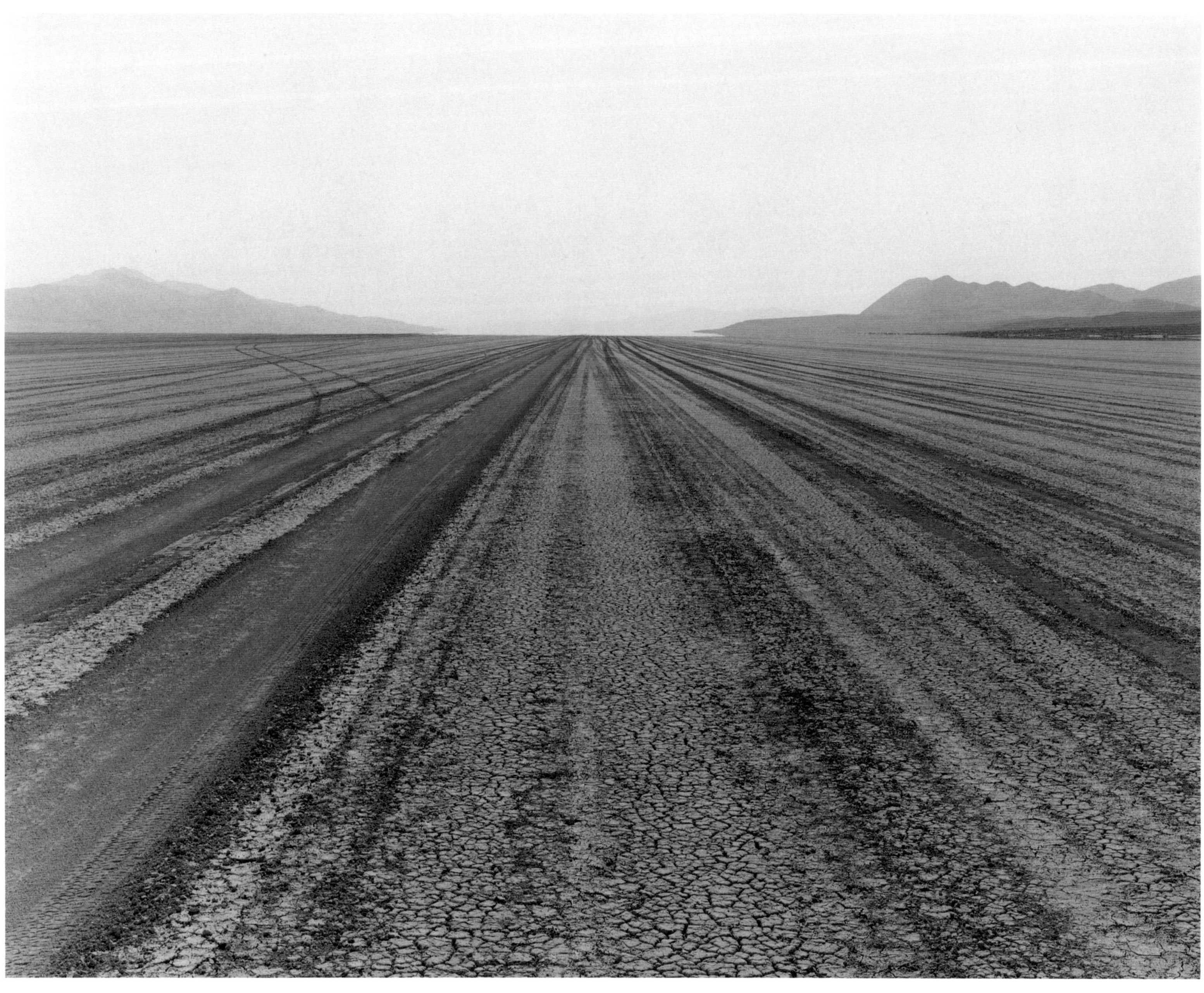

PETER GOIN

25. Black Rock Desert Tracks, Nevada, 1985. (original in color)

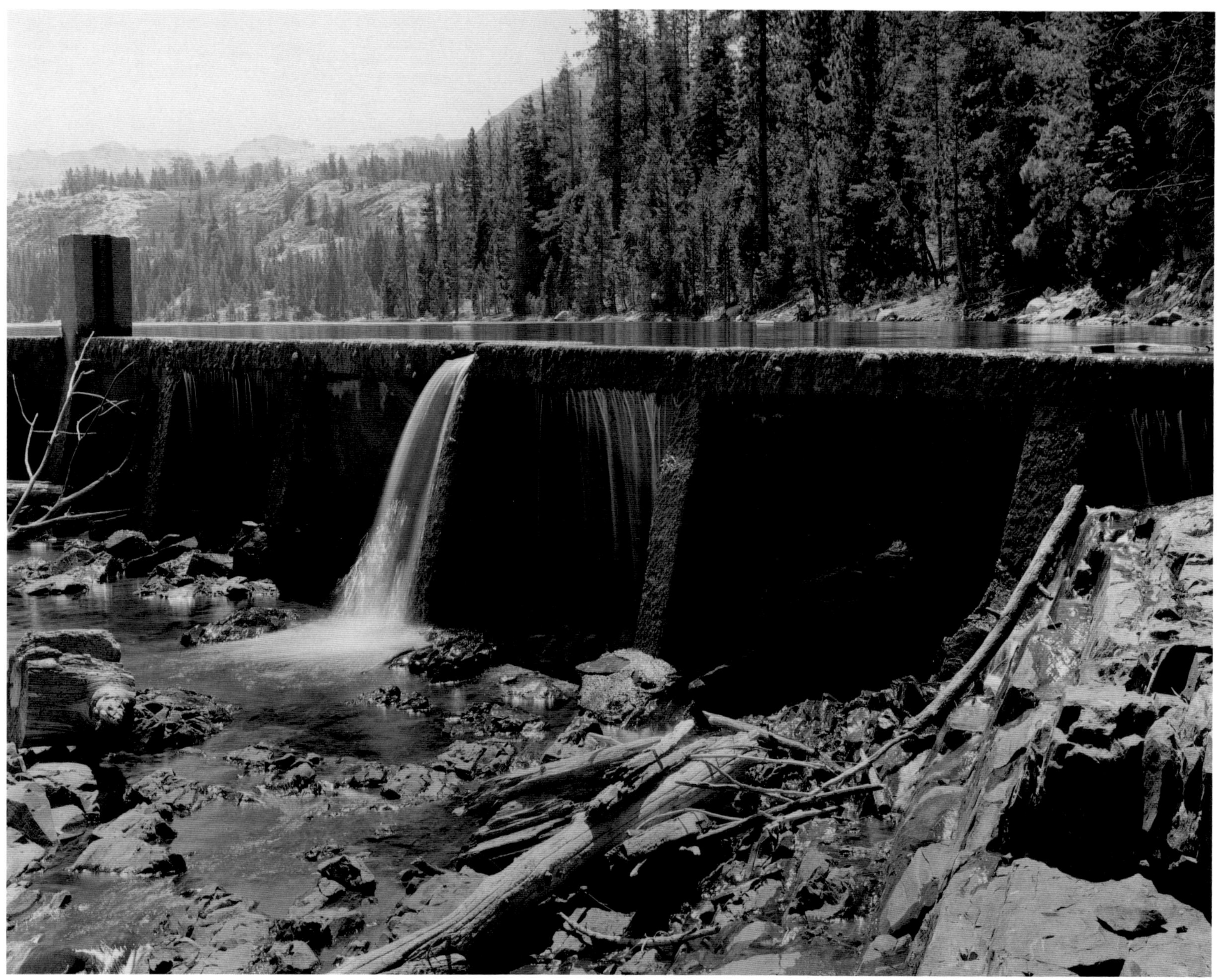

PETER GOIN

26. Sawmill Lake, Sierra Nevada Reservoir, 1990. (original in color)

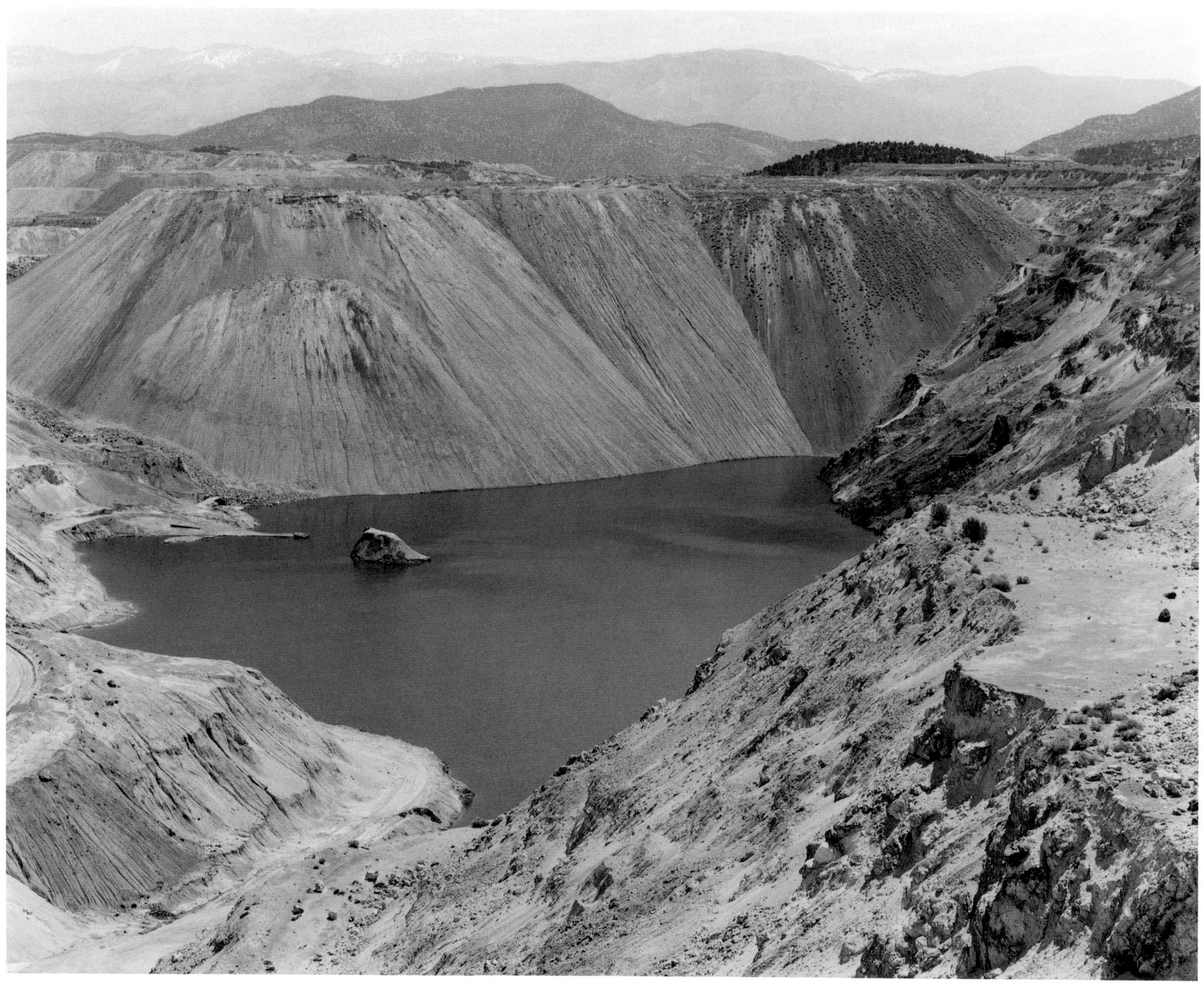

PETER GOIN

27. Abandoned Liberty Pit near Ruth, Nevada, 1986. (original in color)

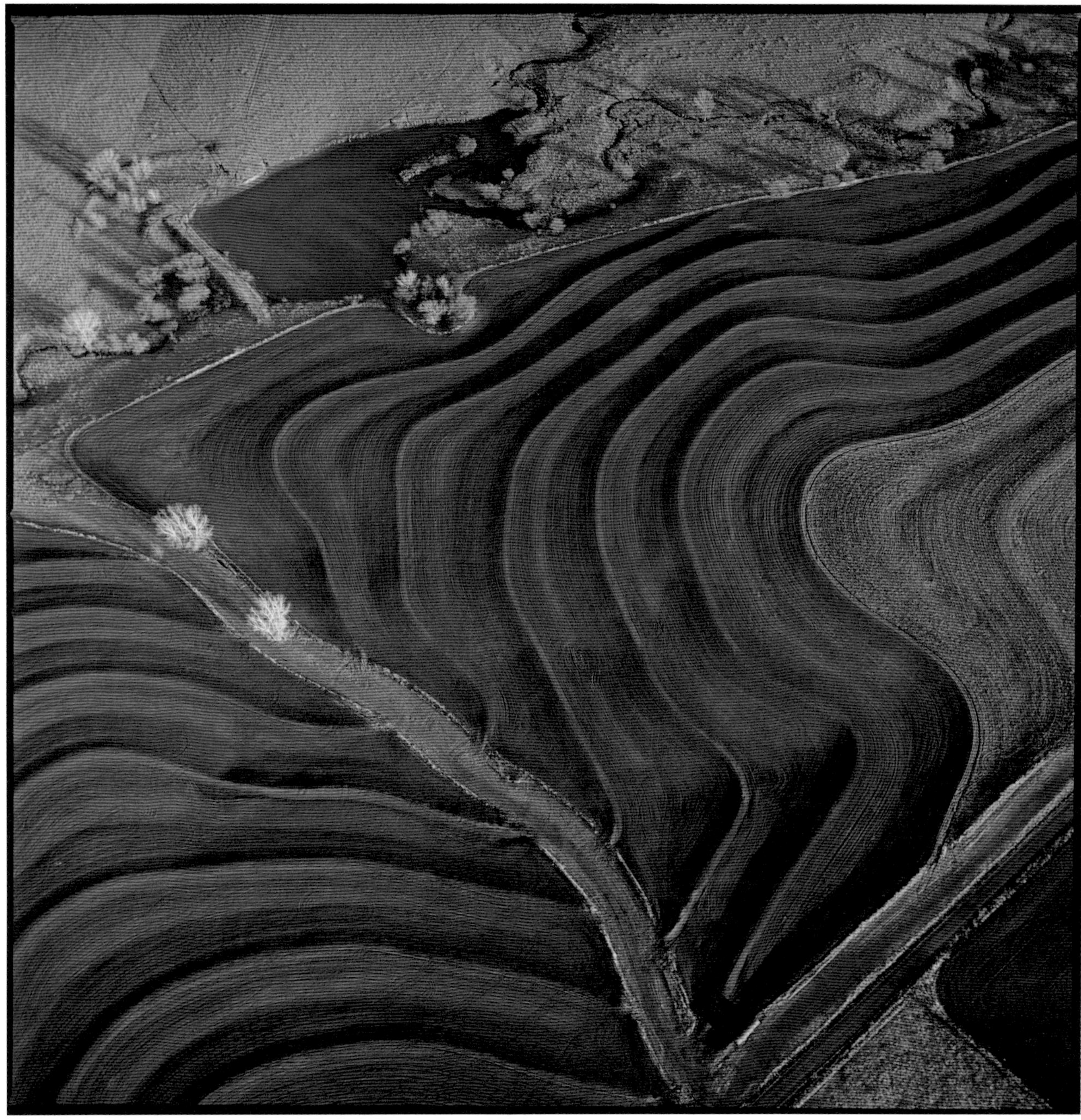

TERRY EVANS

28. Terraced Plowing for Water and Soil Conservation, March 18, 1991.

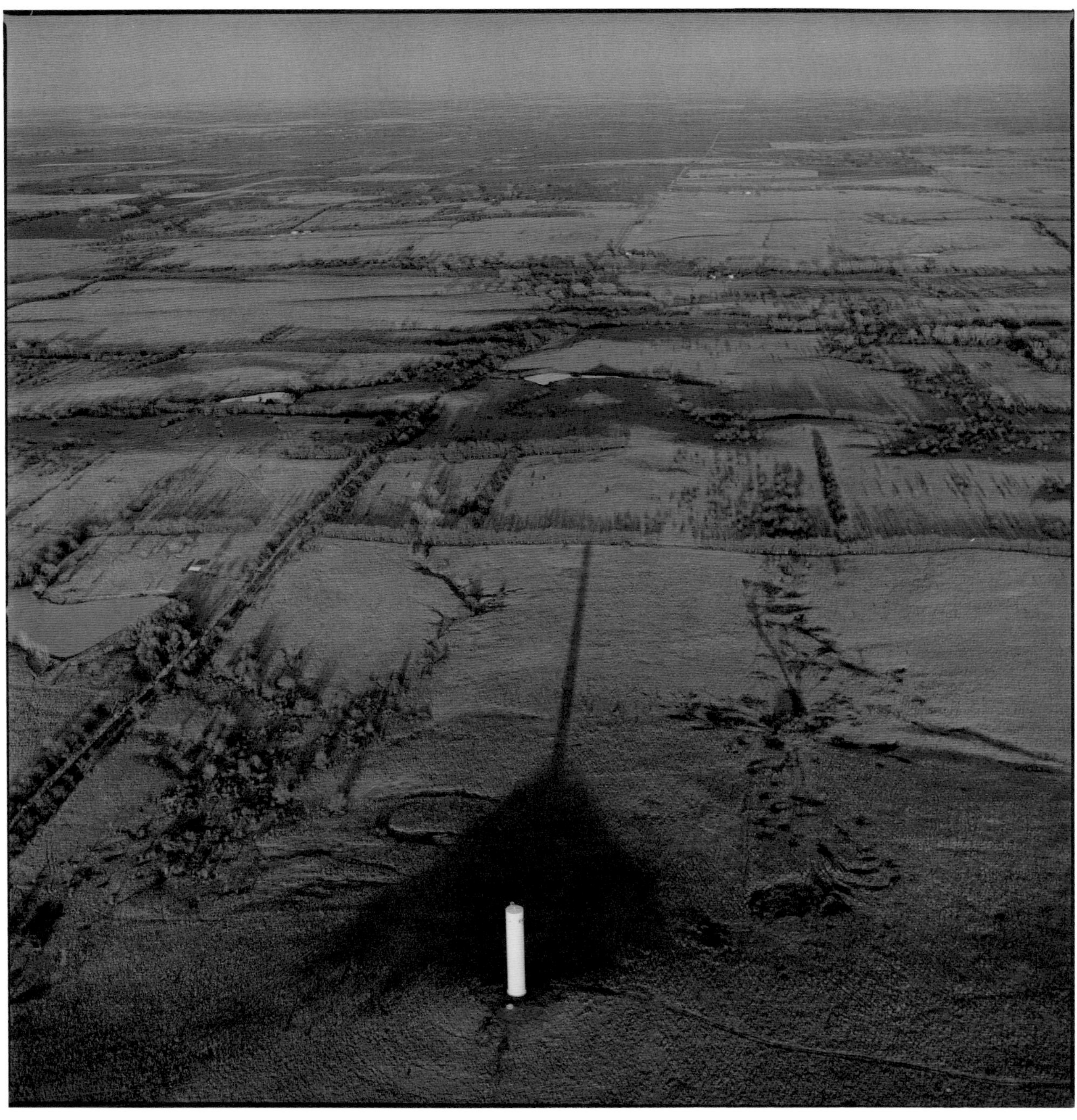

TERRY EVANS

29. Ottawa County, Kansas, Rural Water District #2 Tower, March 18, 1991.

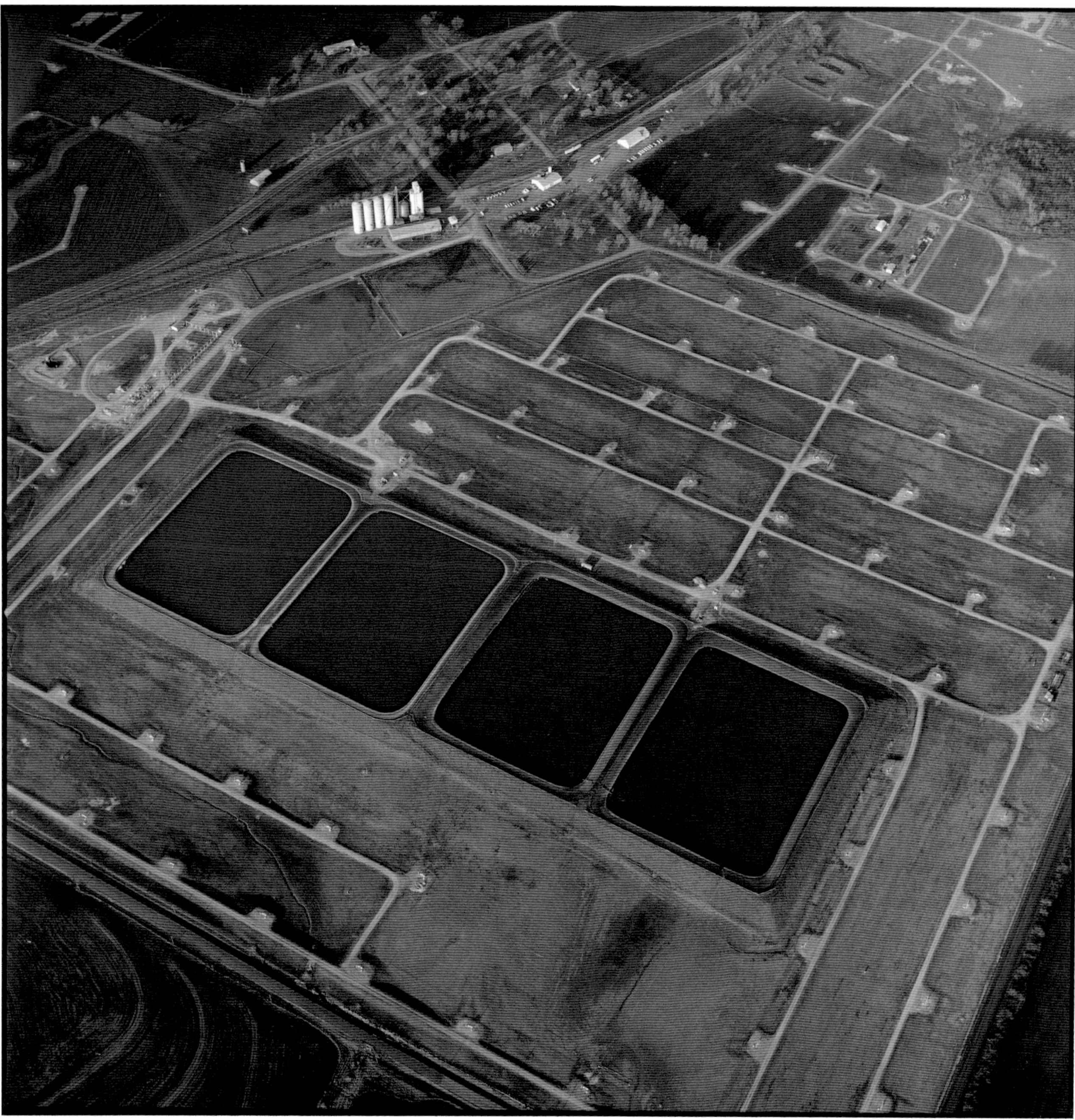

TERRY EVANS

30. Gas Storage Cavities by McPherson, Kansas, March 30, 1991.

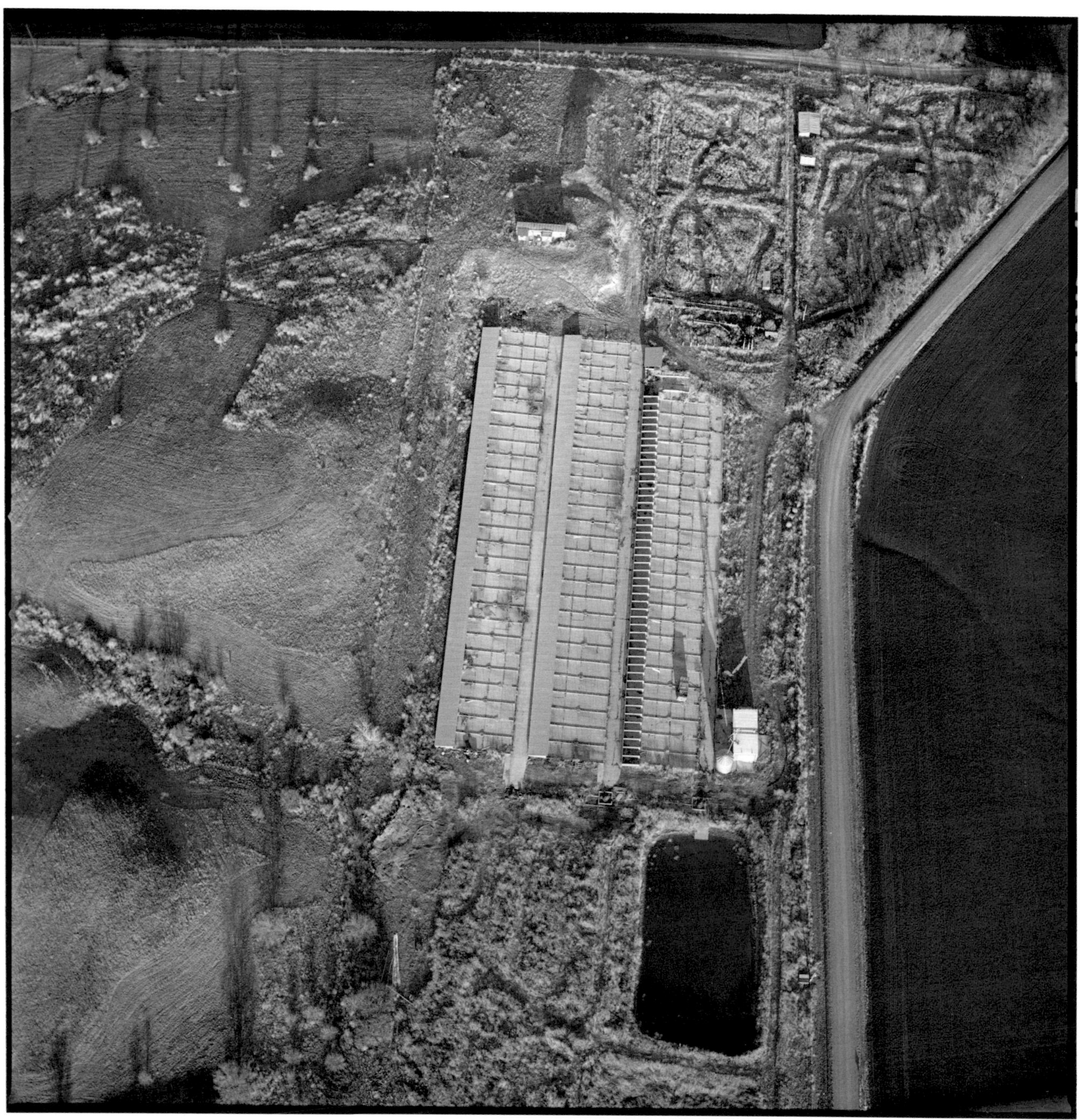

TERRY EVANS

31. Pork Motel, Abandoned Hog Confinement, March 18, 1991.

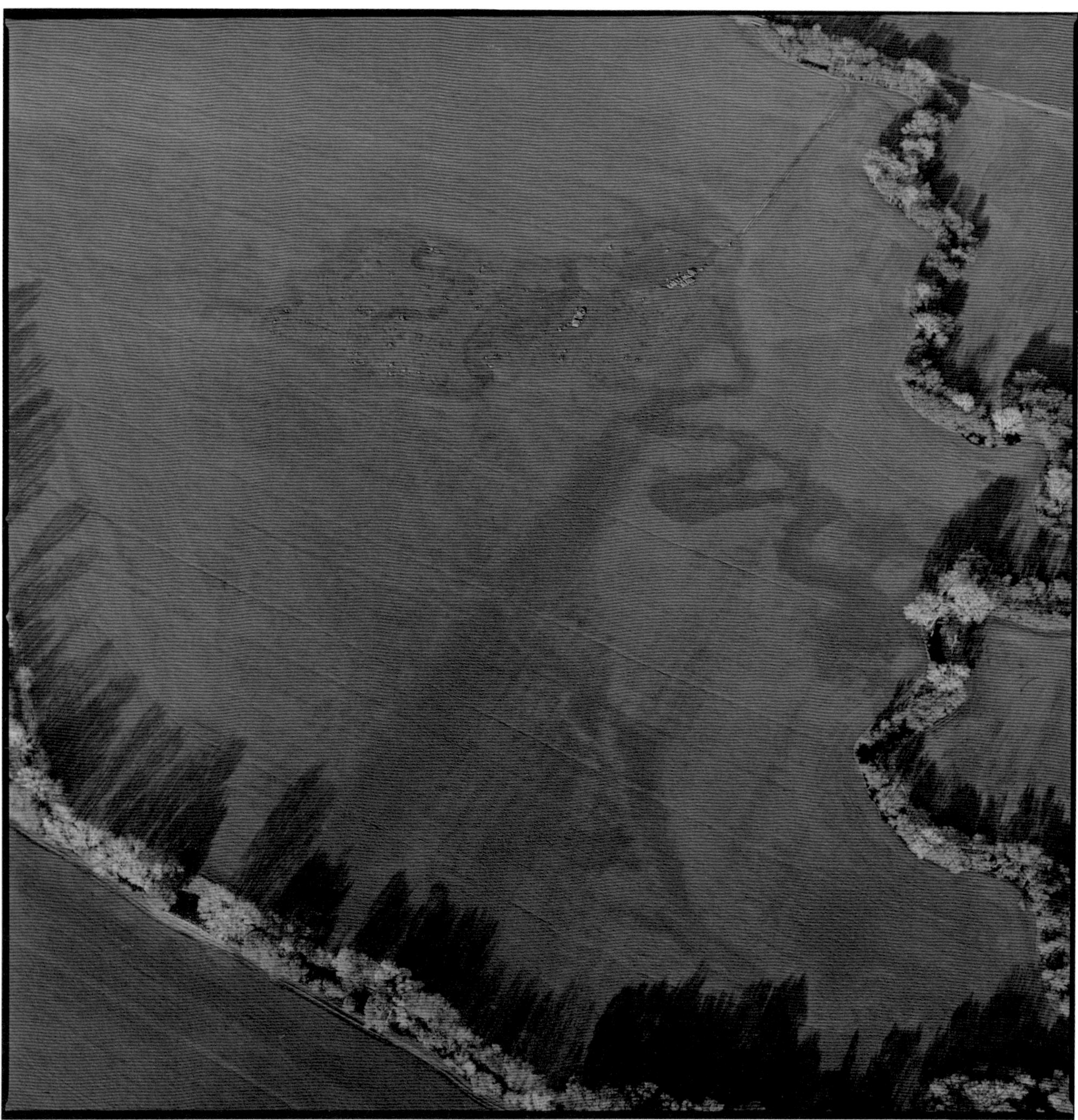

TERRY EVANS

32. Formerly Wichita Indian Village Site, Now a Wheatfield, April 15, 1991.

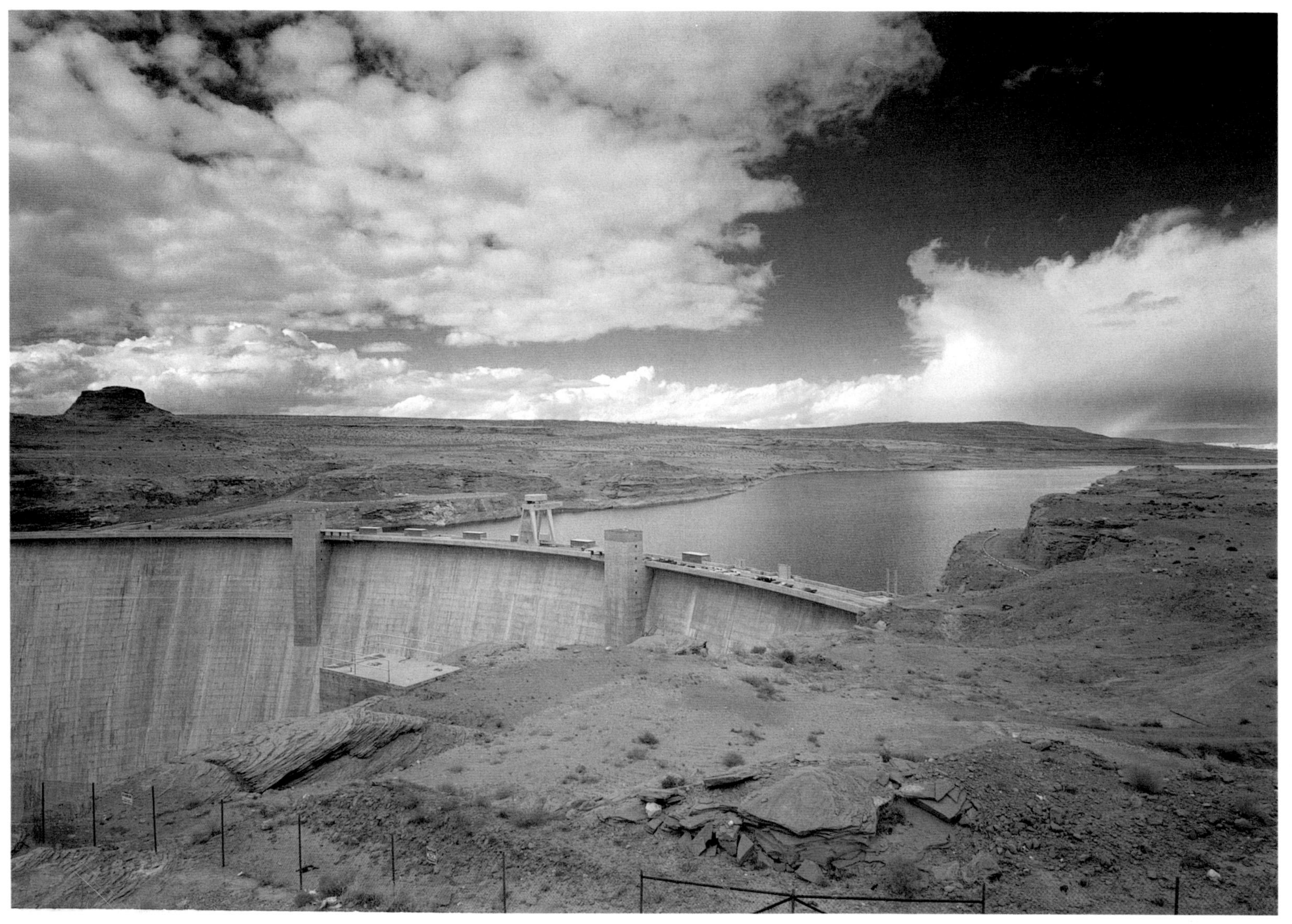

LIVING BEYOND THE RESOURCES

WANDA HAMMERBECK

33. Glen Canyon Dam on the Colorado River—Where there are More Water Rights than Water, 1991.

(original in color)

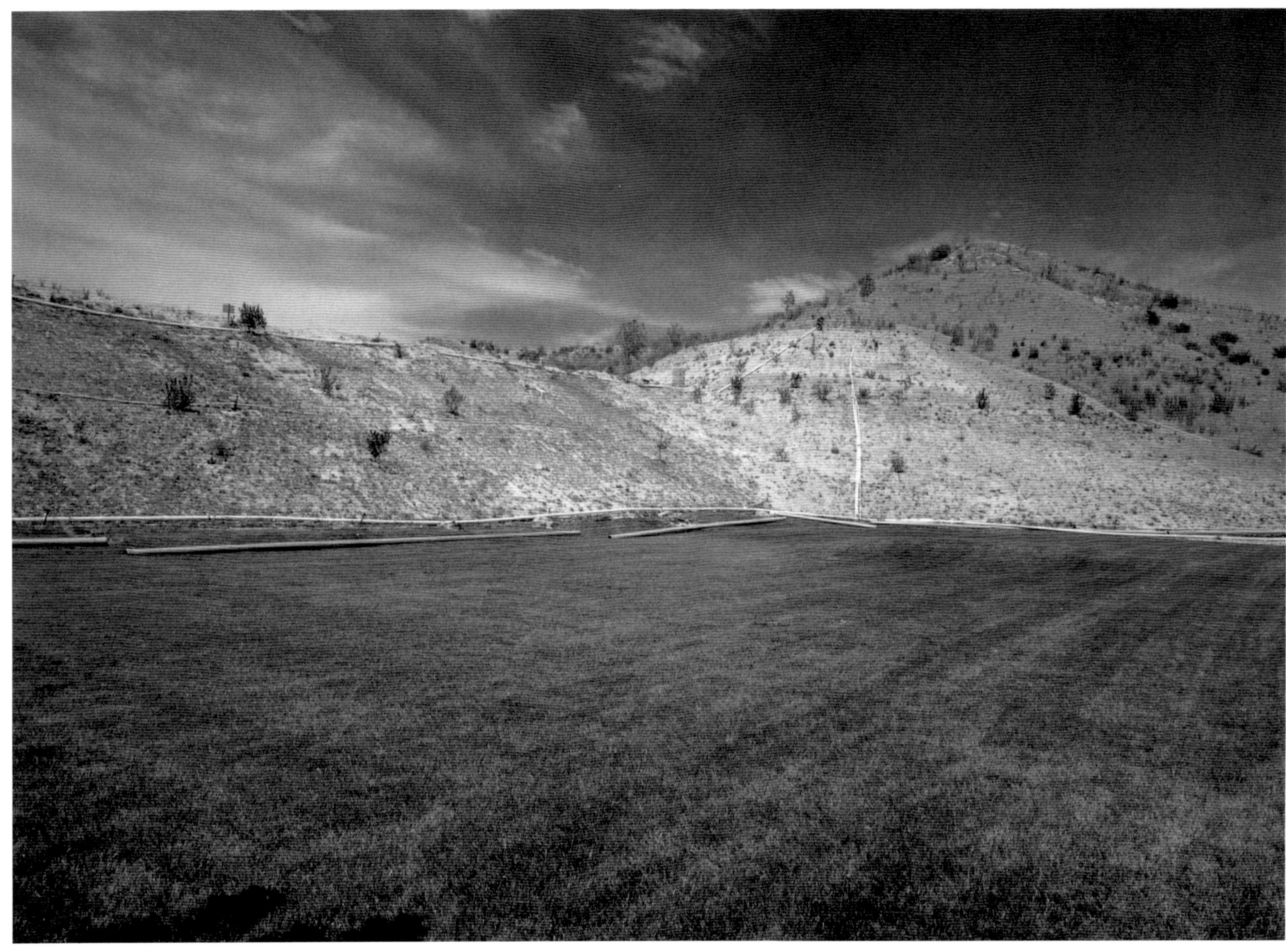

WANDA HAMMERBECK

34. Imposing an Eastern Idea of Lawn in a Desert Housing Development near Los Angeles, 1991. (original in color)

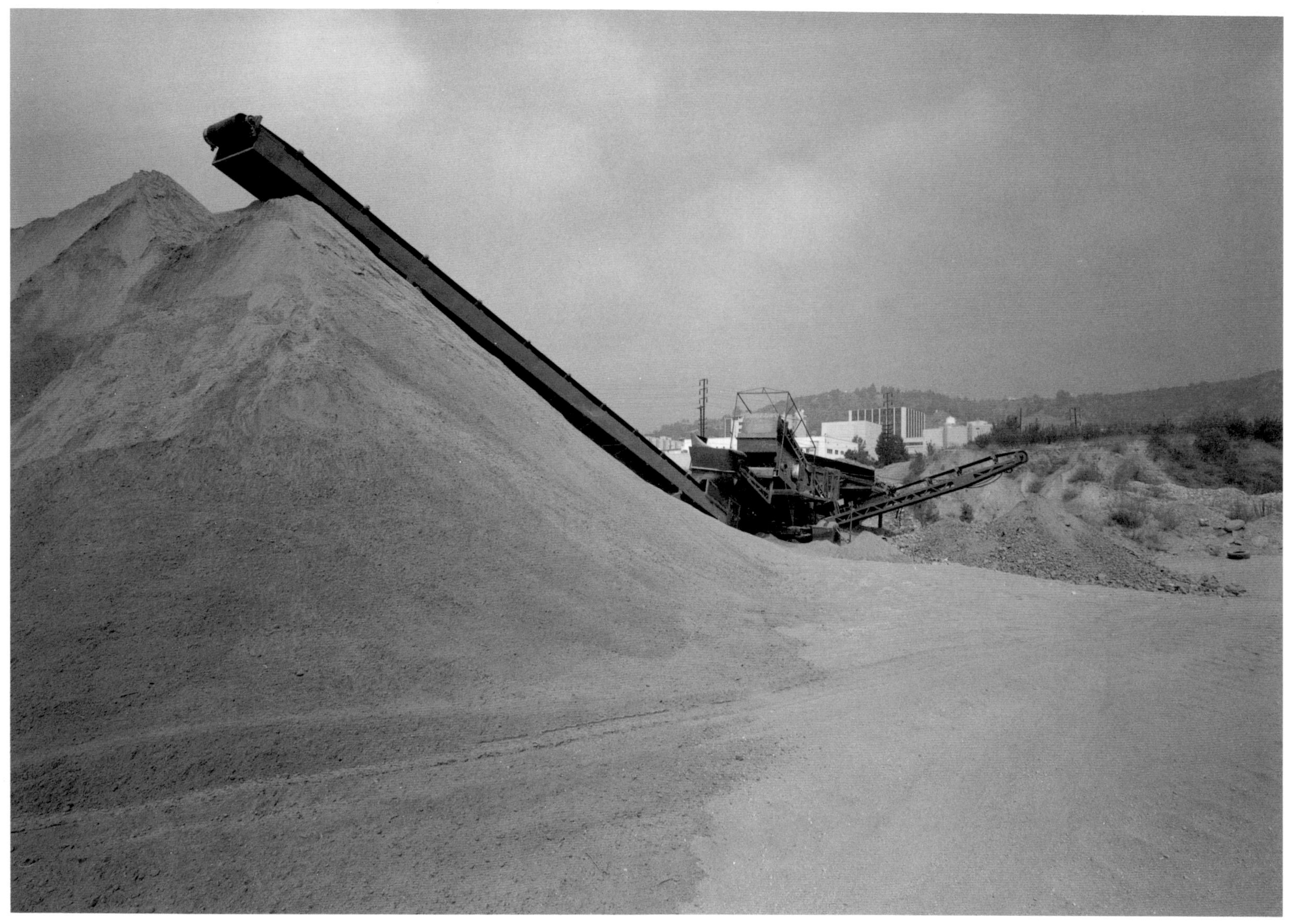

SILT EXCAVATION BEHIND DEVIL'S GATE DAM

WANDA HAMMERBECK

35. Devil's Gate Dam in the Arroyo Seco, Flintridge, California. NASA Jet Propulsion Laboratory in Background, 1991.

(original in color)

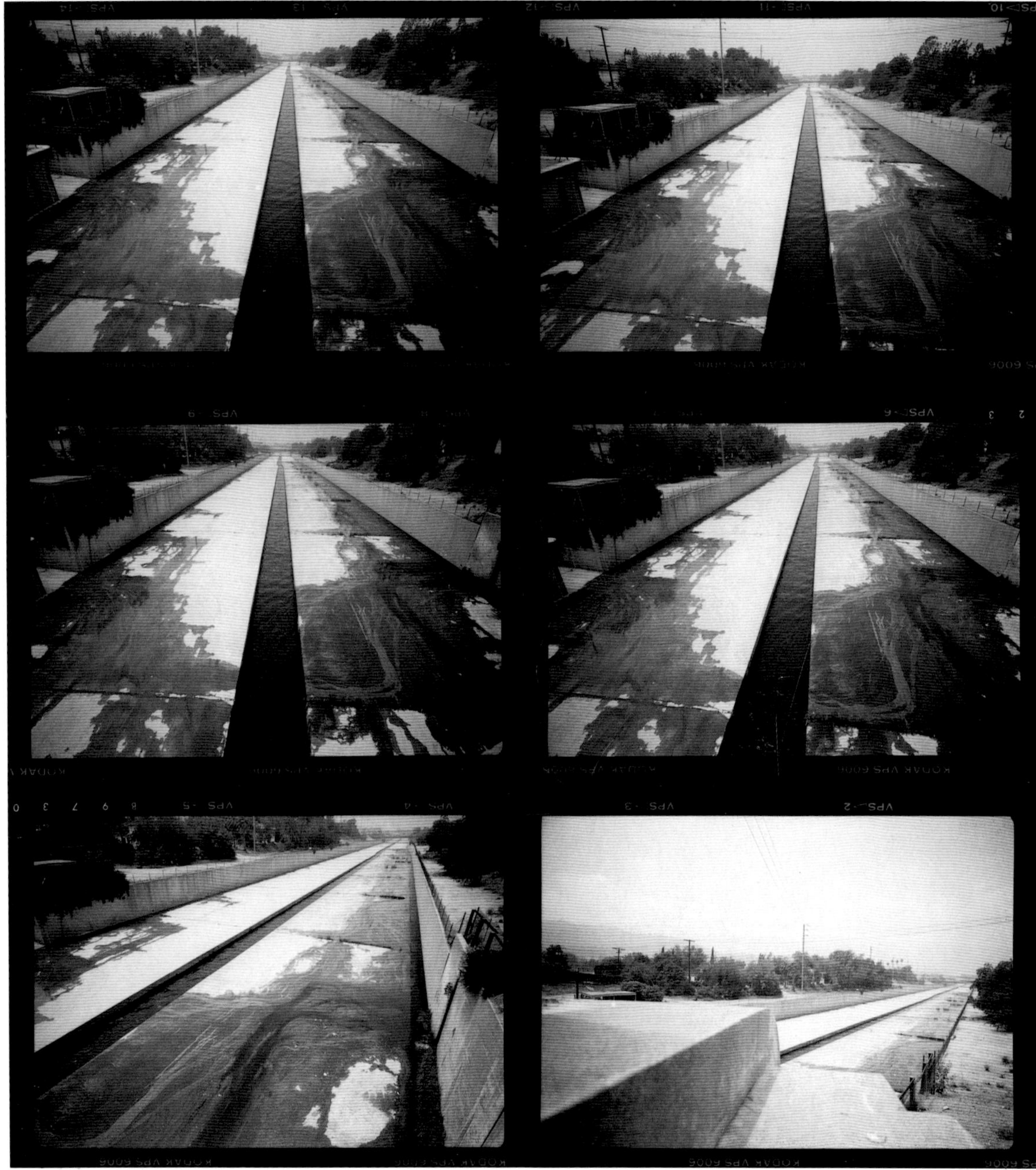

WANDA HAMMERBECK

36. From the Series Entitled: The Los Angeles: A River Controlled, 1991.

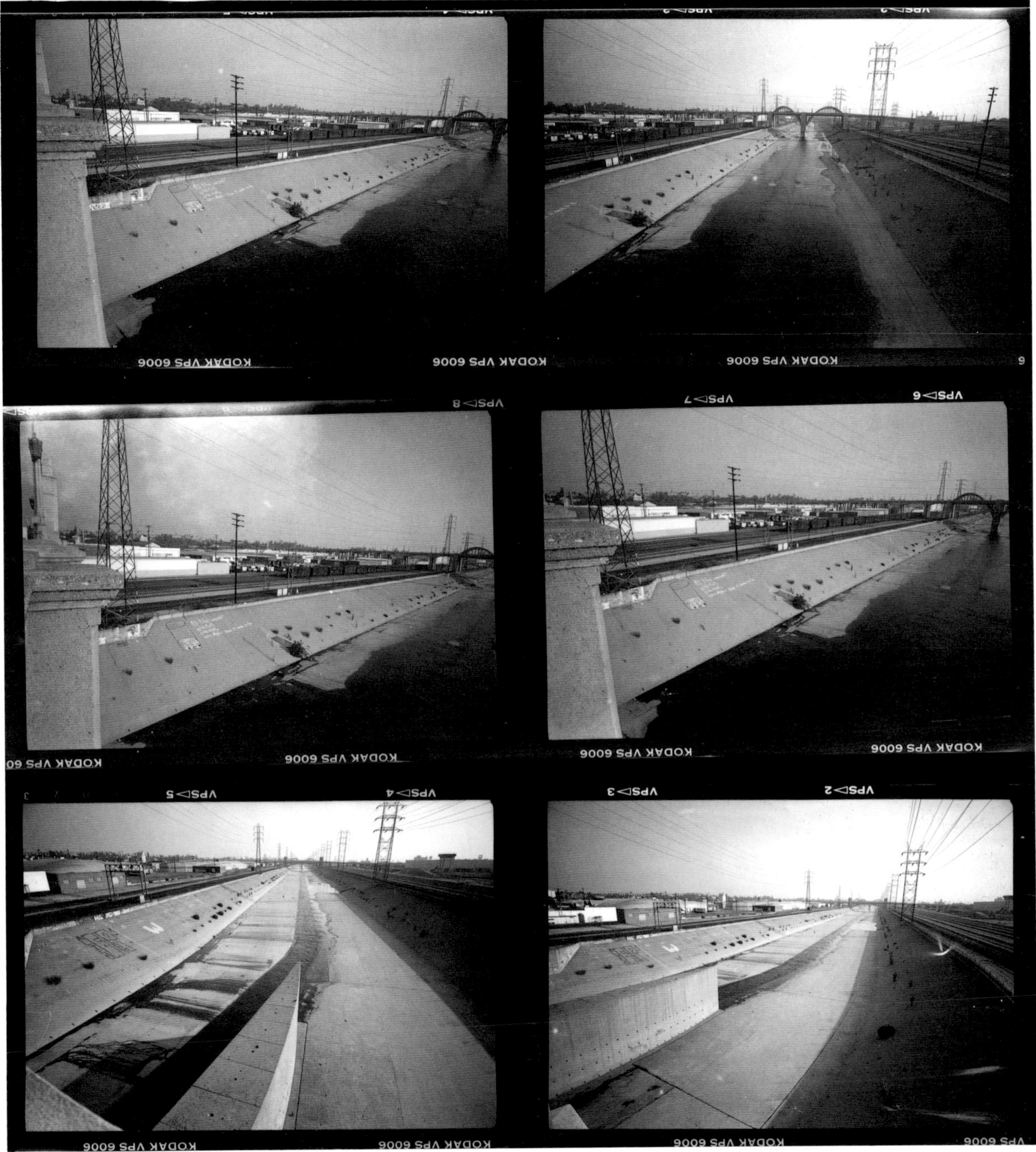

WANDA HAMMERBECK

37. From the Series Entitled: The Los Angeles: A River Controlled, 1991.

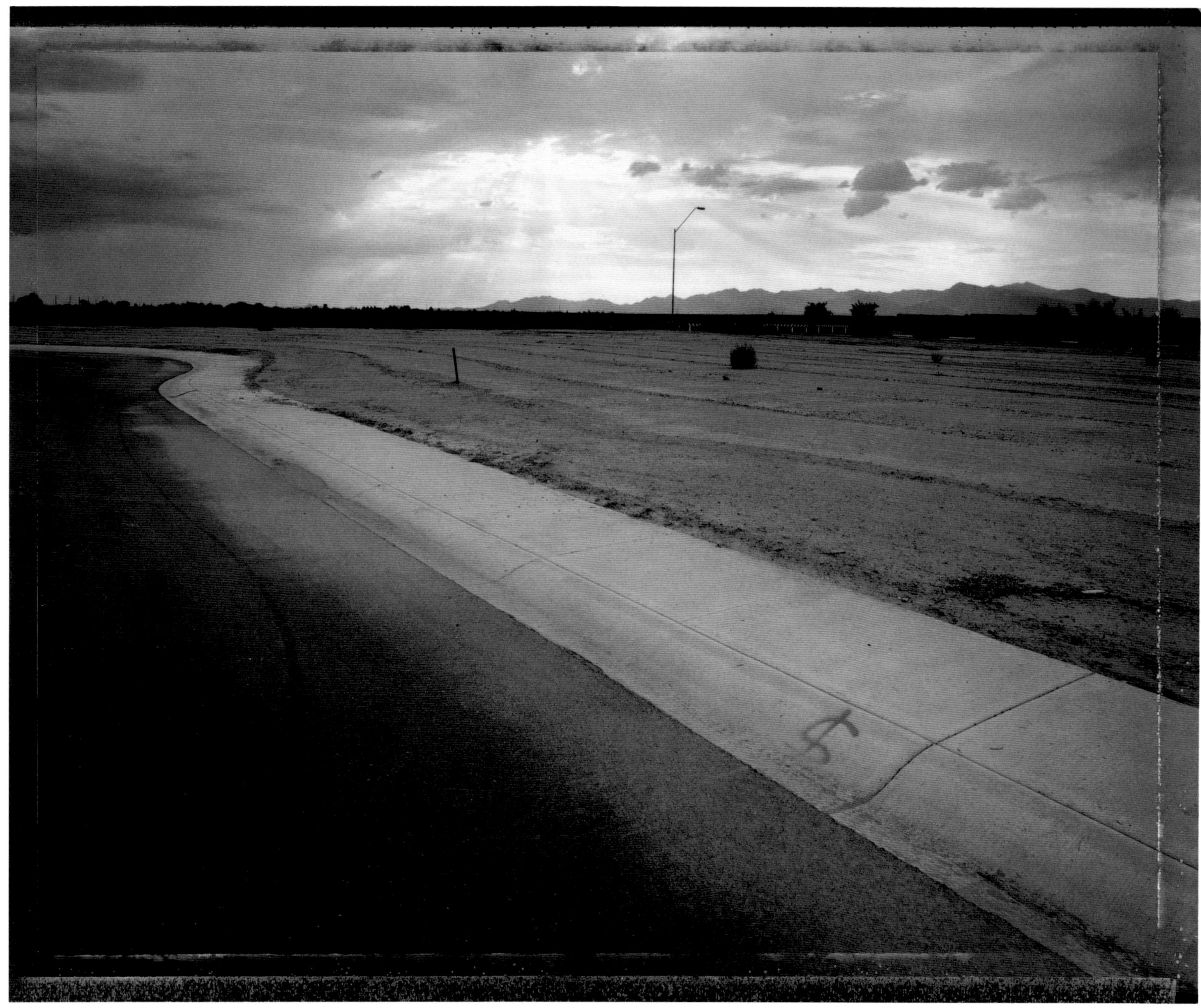

MARK KLETT

38. Undeveloped Lot on Hilton Street, "Estrella Vista," 7/16/90.

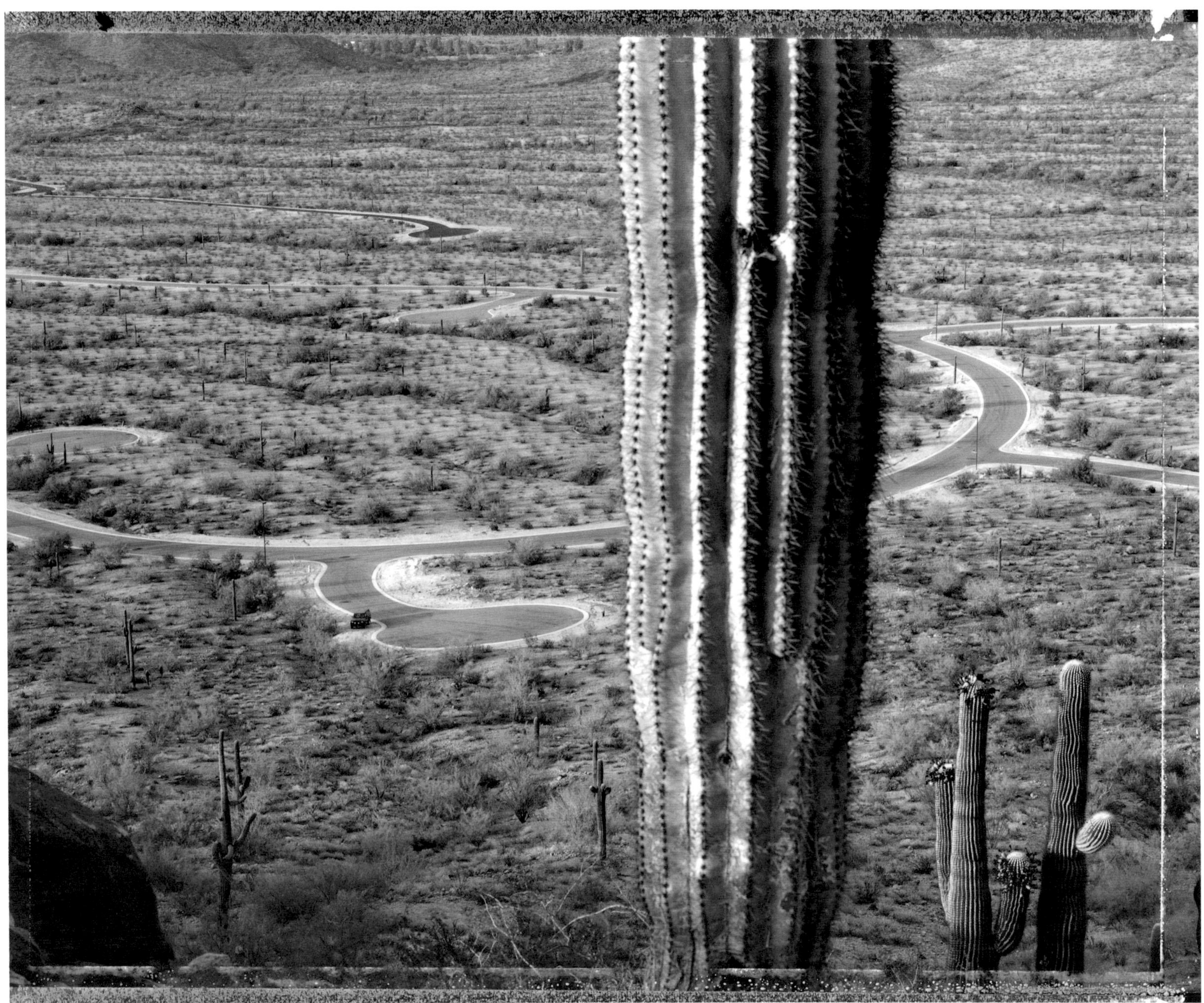

MARK KLETT

39. Cul de Sacs: Failed Development, "Estrella," 7/17/90.

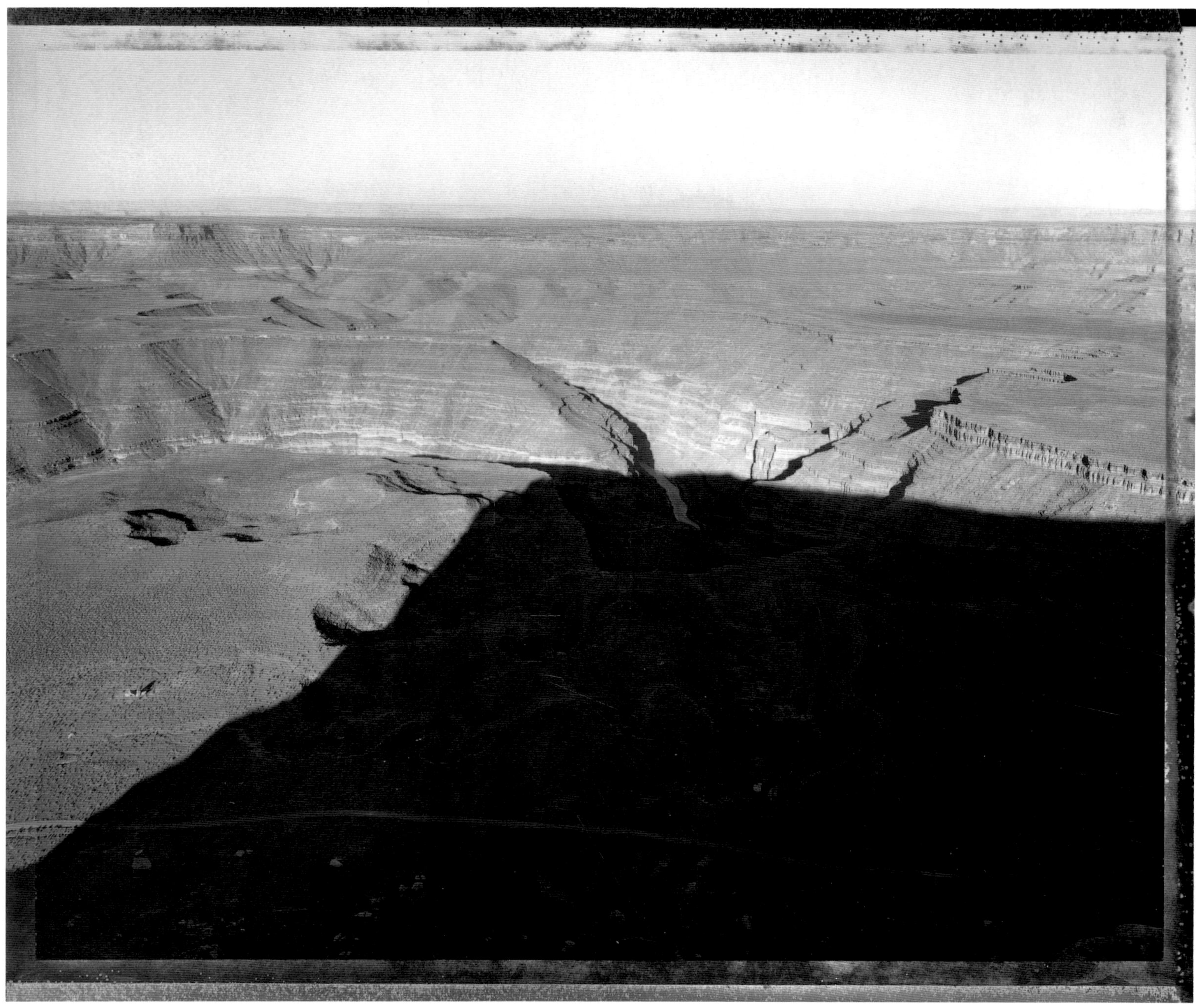

MARK KLETT

40. Intersection of Muley Point's Shadow and the San Juan River, 7:35 A.M., 5/23/91.

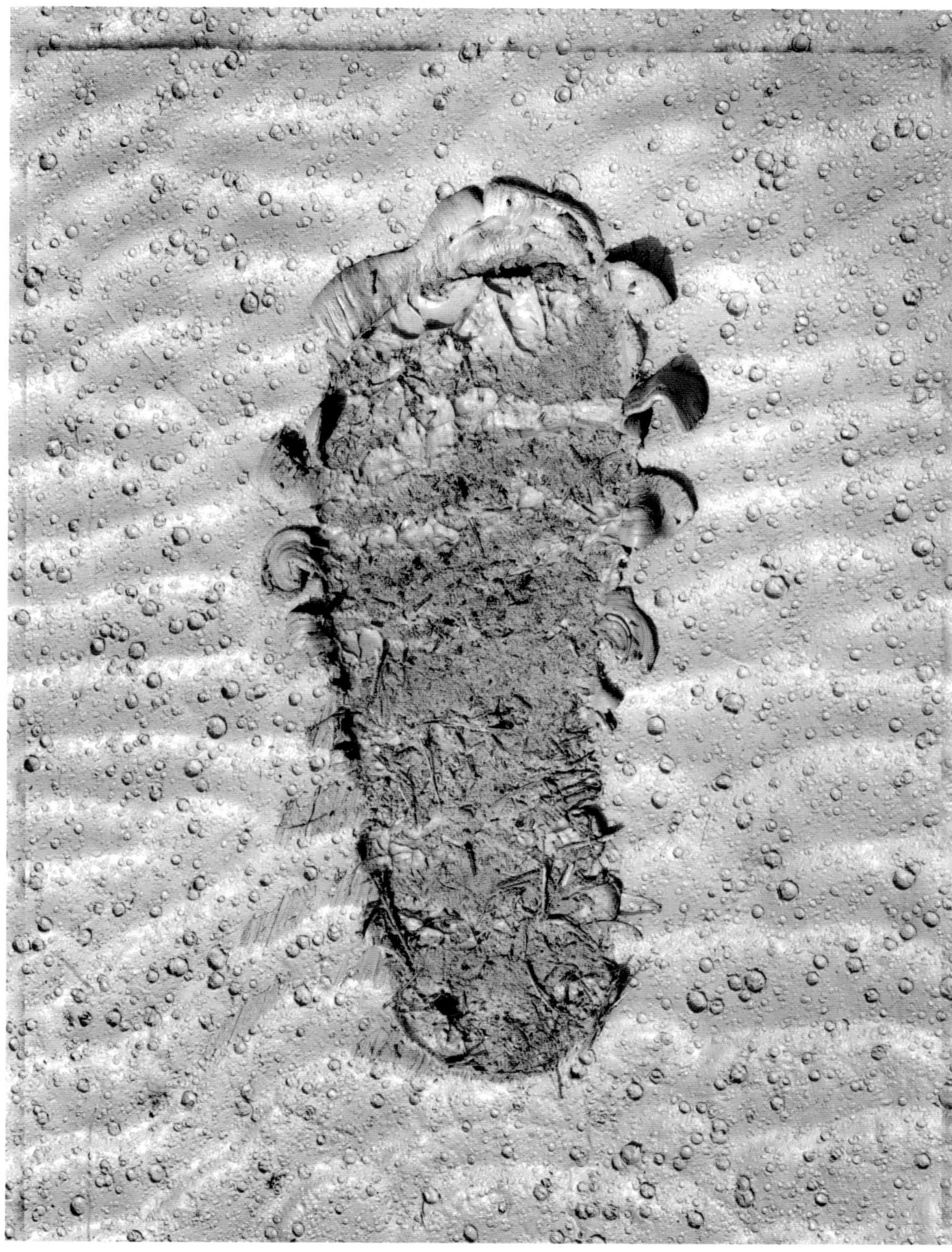

MARK KLETT

41. Boatman's Sandal Print, San Juan River, 9/27/90.

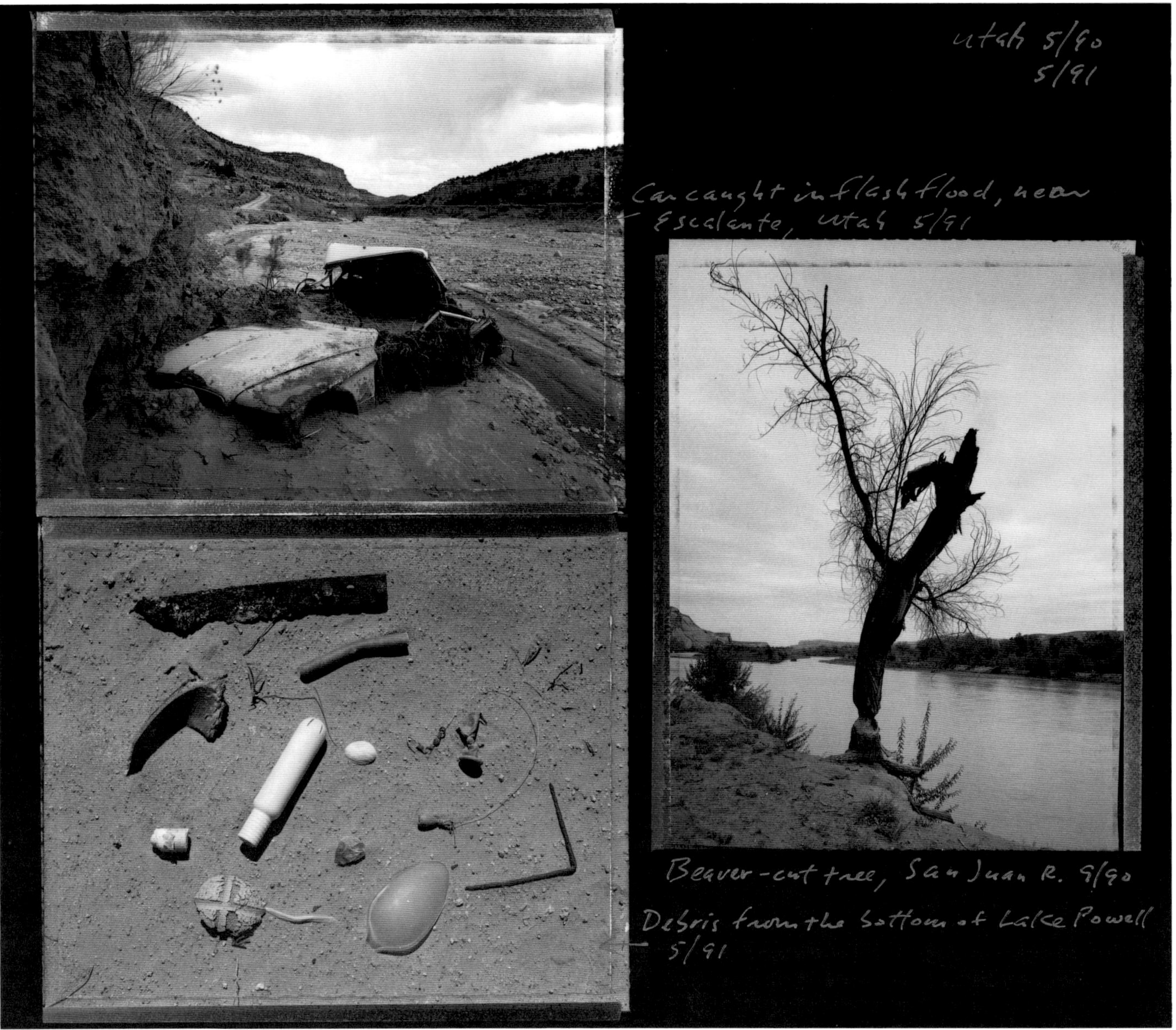

MARK KLETT

42A. Car Caught in Flash Flood, near Escalante, Utah, 5/91.

42B. Debris from the Bottom of Lake Powell, 5/91.

42C. Beaver-cut Tree, San Juan River, 9/90.

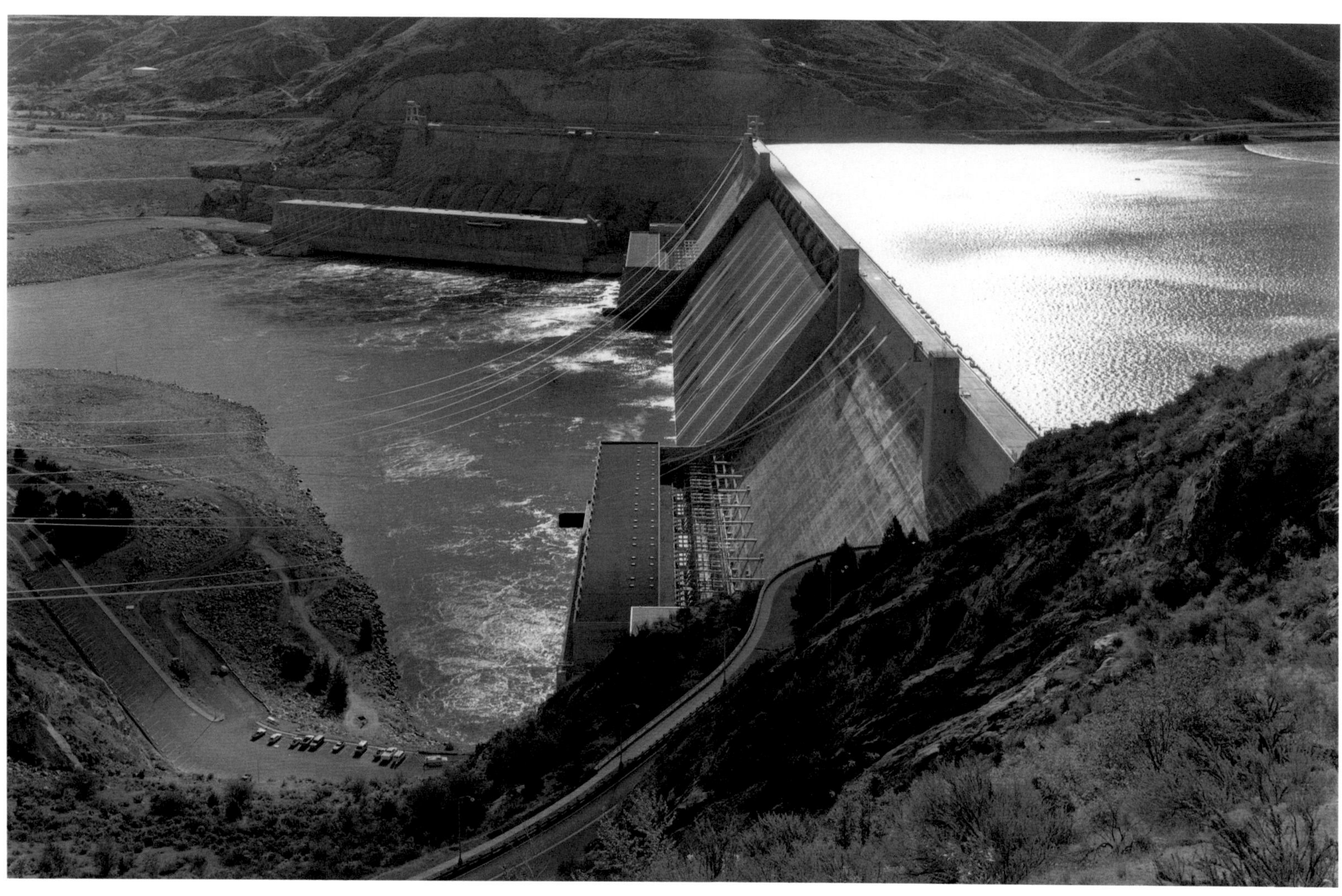

MARTIN STUPICH

43. Columbia Basin Project, Grand Coulee Dam, 1991.

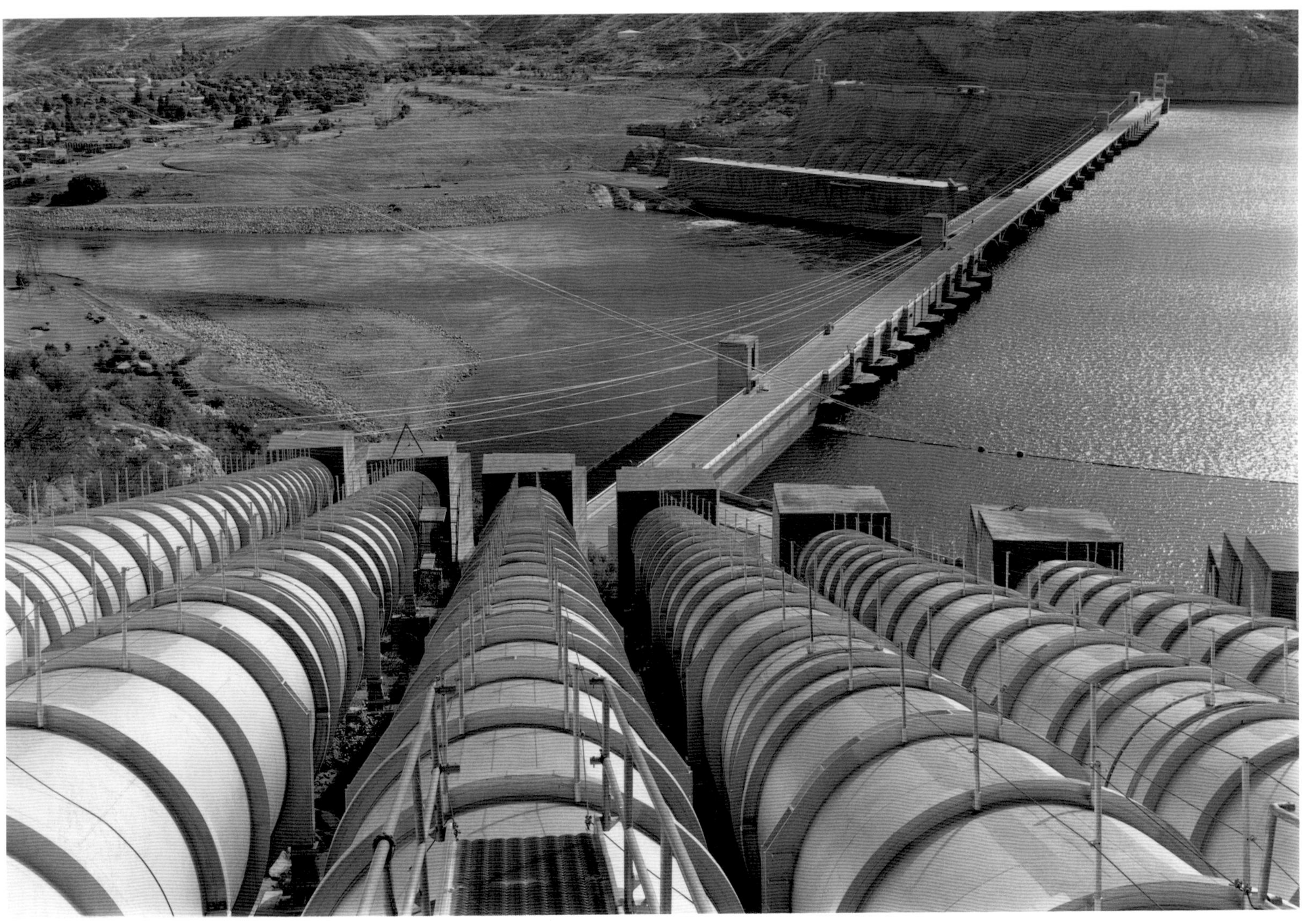

MARTIN STUPICH

44. Columbia Basin Project, Siphon Discharge Pipes, Grand Coulee Dam, 1991.

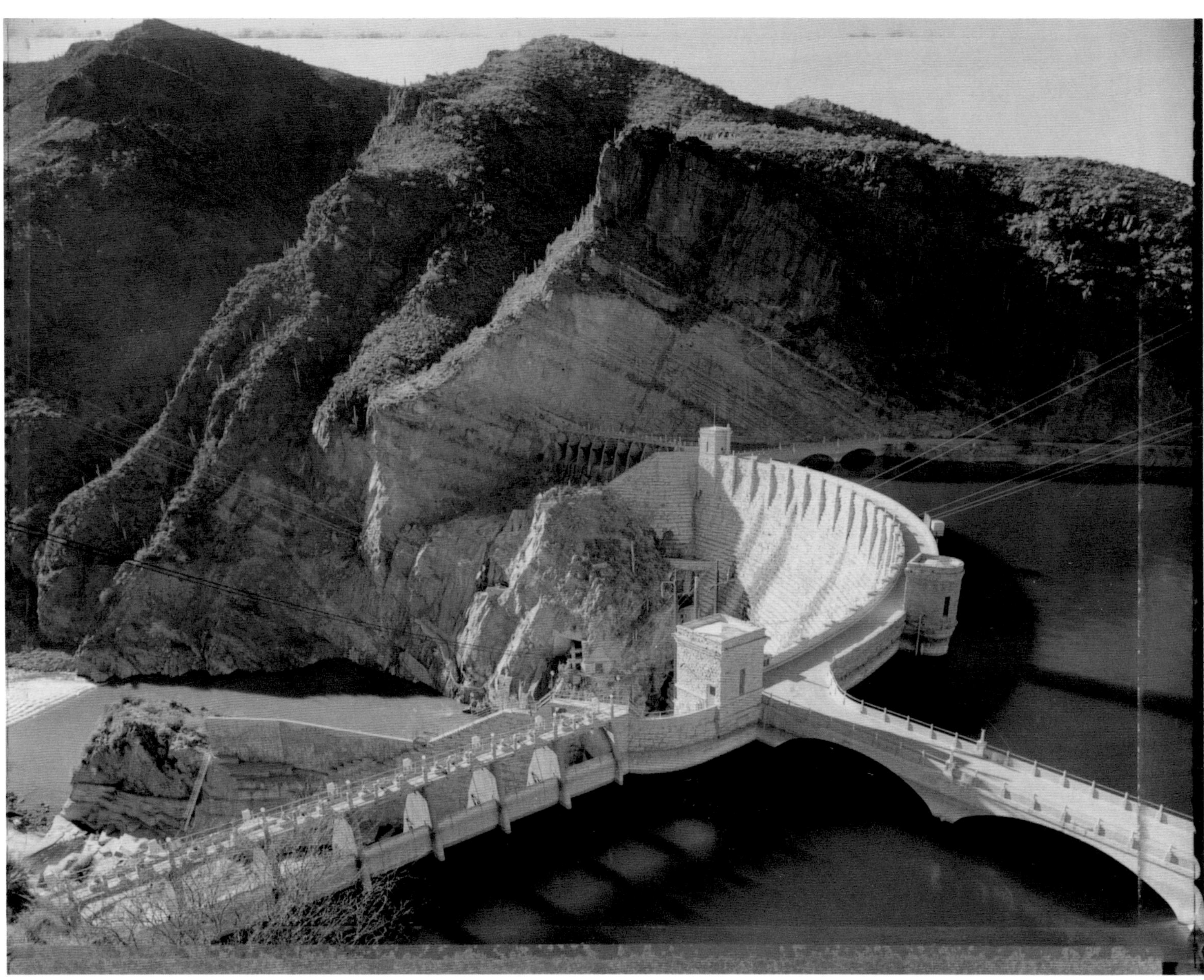

MARTIN STUPICH

45. Theodore Roosevelt Dam, Arizona, 1988.

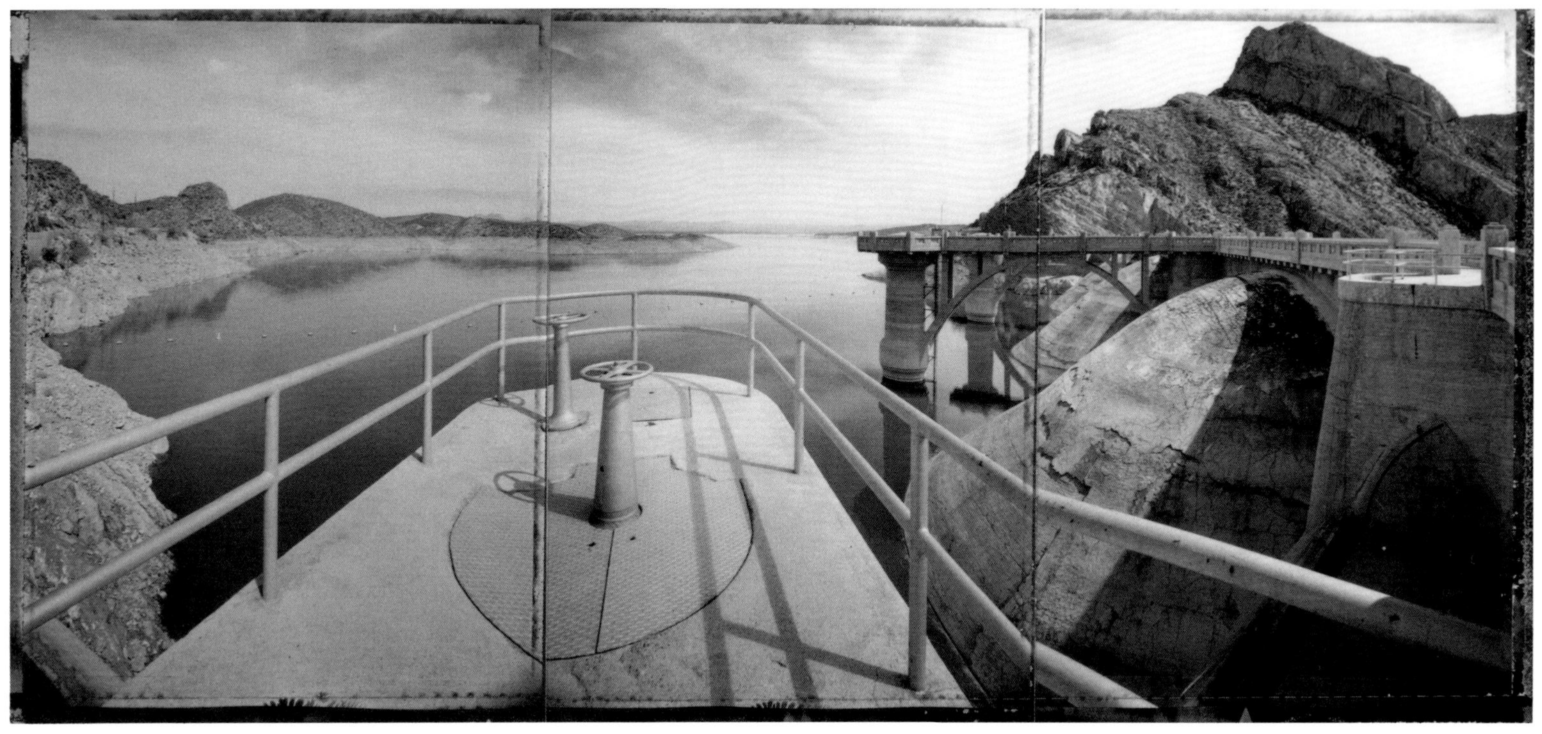

MARTIN STUPICH

46. San Carlos Reservoir and Coolidge Dam, Arizona, 1988.

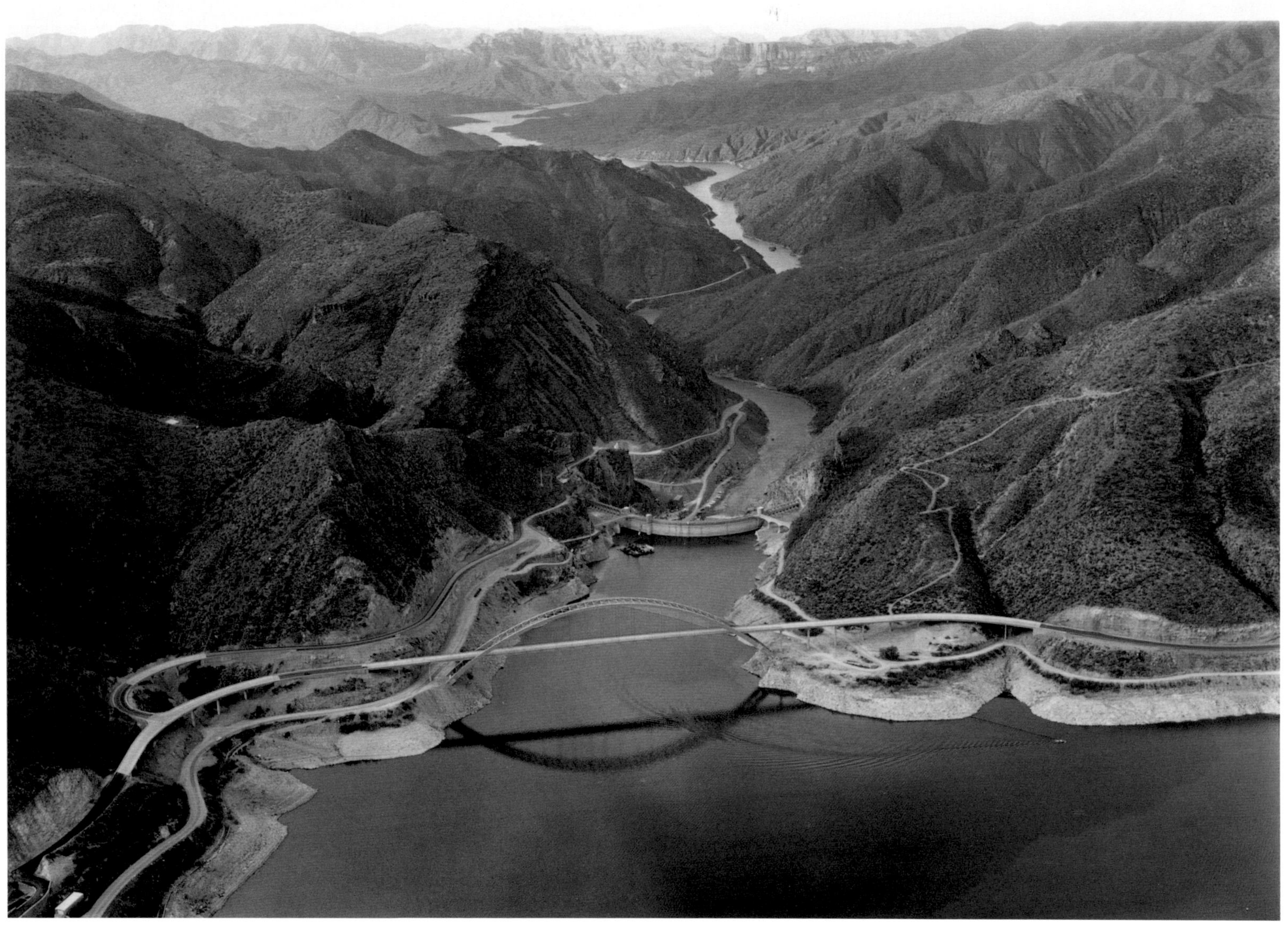

MARTIN STUPICH

47. Aerial View, Roosevelt Lake, Bridge, and Dam, 1991.

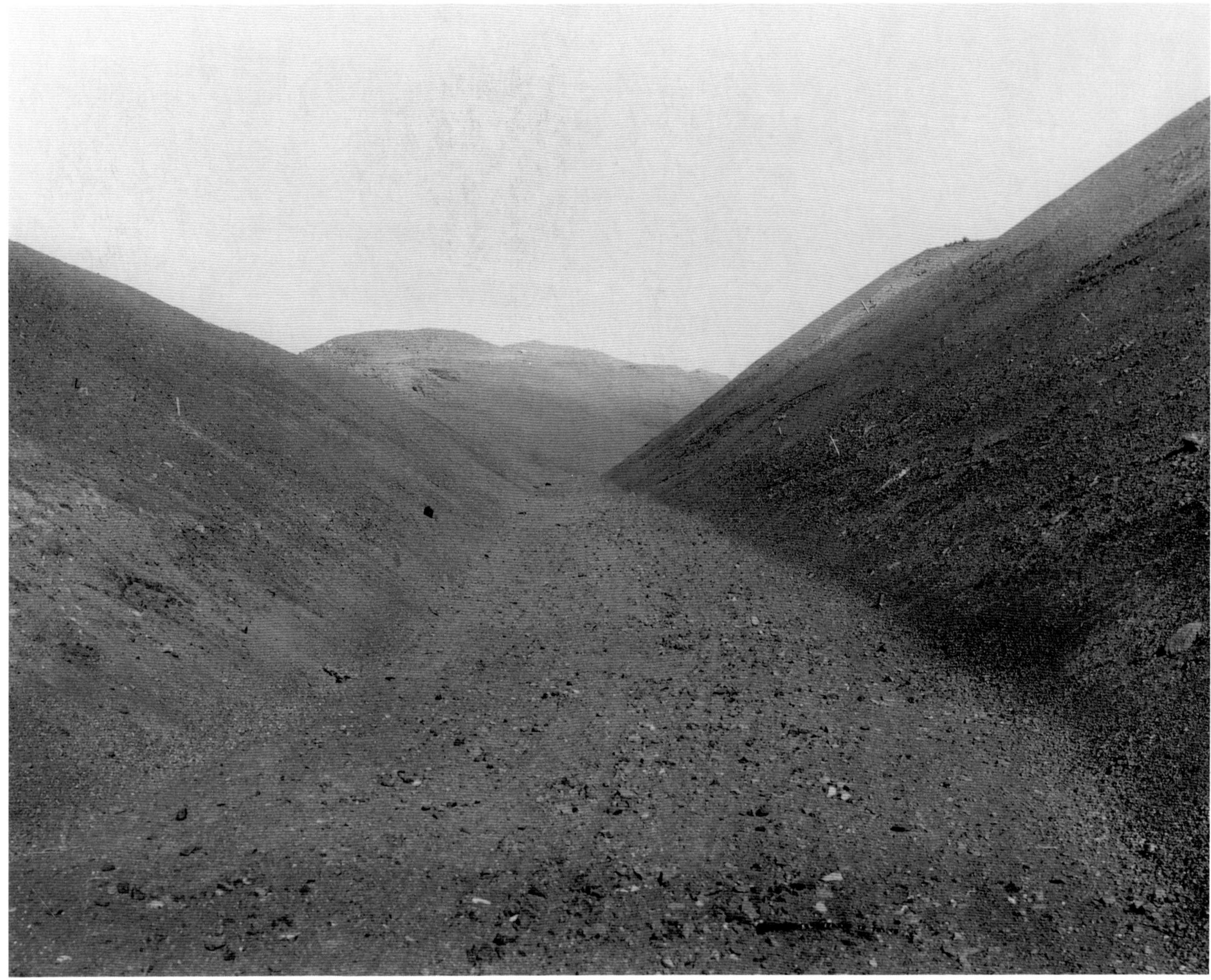

PHOTOGRAPHER UNIDENTIFIED

48. Work being done on Truckee Canal, part of the Truckee-Carson Irrigation Project, Nevada, ca. 1905.

Courtesy of the Special Collections Department, University of Nevada, Reno, Library.

ACKNOWLEDGMENTS

Without the support of the following individuals and institutions, this project may never have been completed: Marian Allen, Robert E. Blesse, William Cathey, Jayna Conkey, Steve Davis, Robert Dawson, Jennifer Dowley, Joe Ely, the Exhibition Committee in the Art Department at the University of Nevada, Reno, Headlands Center for the Arts, Kenneth Helphand, Scott Hilton, Wayne Horn, Taffy Johnson, Jessica Ledbetter, Jim McCormick, Walter McNamara, Marilyn Melton, Chelsea Miller, Elizabeth Morris, Joan Morrow, Marianne Murray, Nevada Humanities Committee, Paul Page, Reed Powers, Thomas Radko, Ann Ronald, Tami Scronce, Sheppard Gallery, Sierra Arts Foundation, Tom Southall, Richard Squalia, Jane Stenehjem, the University of Nevada, Reno, Todd Warnock, Judy Winzeler, Don Worster, and finally, the photographers in the Water in the West Project.

PARTICIPANT BIOGRAPHIES

LAURIE BROWN

SELECTED PUBLICATIONS: *A River Too Far*, Nevada Humanities Committee and University of Nevada Press, 1991; *Picturing California: A Century of Photographic Genius*, The Oakland Museum/Chronicle Books, 1989; *EARTH-EDGES*, 1984 (portfolio); **Centric 6: Laurie Brown*, University Art Museum, Long Beach, 1983; *Target III: In Sequence*, The Houston Museum of Fine Arts, 1982; *LA Issue*, LACPS, 1979 (portfolio); *WESTCOASTNOW*, 1979 (portfolio). SELECTED EXHIBITIONS: "The Water in the West Project," University of Nevada, Reno, 1991; "Changing Realities," Sezon Museum, Tokyo, 1991; *Jan Turner Gallery, Los Angeles, 1989; "Picturing California: A Century of Photographic Genius," The Oakland Museum, 1989; *Palm Springs Desert Museum, 1988; "Facets of the Collection," San Francisco Museum of Modern Art, 1987; "Photomosaics: The Landscape Reconstructed," The Photographic Resource Center, Boston, 1986; *Arco Center for the Visual Arts, Los Angeles, 1978. AWARDS AND GRANTS: National Endowment for the Arts Visual Artists' Fellowship, 1978. EDUCATION: MA, California State University, Fullerton; BA, Scripps College. Currently resides in Laguna Beach, California.

*Denotes monograph or one-person exhibition.

GREGORY CONNIFF

SELECTED PUBLICATIONS: *A River Too Far*, Nevada Humanities Committee and University of Nevada Press, 1991; *Gregory Conniff/Frank Gohlke: Two Days in Louisiana*, Milwaukee Museum of Art, 1989; **Common Ground*, Yale University Press, 1985; **Gregory Conniff*, Corcoran Gallery of Art, 1979. SELECTED EXHIBITIONS: "The Water in the West Project," University of Nevada, Reno, 1991; *Akron Art Museum, Akron, Ohio; *Corcoran Gallery of Art; *Madison Art Center; *Museum of Contemporary Photography, Chicago; *Toledo Museum of Art; Baltimore Museum of Art; Fogg Art Museum; Museum of Fine Arts, Boston; High Museum, Atlanta. AWARDS AND GRANTS: Wisconsin Arts Board, Visual Arts Fellowship, 1990, 1983, 1979; Guggenheim Fellowship, 1989; National Endowment for the Arts Visual Artists' Fellowship, 1981. RELATED WORK EXPERIENCE: Attorney on law in art and publishing; consultant and lecturer on art and law; VISTA volunteer, Atlanta. EDUCATION: LL.B. University of Virginia School of Law; BA, Columbia University. Further studies at the University of Wisconsin Graduate School of Art. Currently resides in Madison, Wisconsin.

ROBERT DAWSON

SELECTED PUBLICATIONS: *The Great Central Valley Project*, University of California Press, Berkeley, 1992; *A River*

Too Far, Nevada Humanities Committee and University of Nevada Press, 1991; *Aperture #120*, Fall 1990; *Mother Jones*, April/May, 1990; *Picturing California: A Century of Photographic Genius*, The Oakland Museum, 1989; **Robert Dawson Photographs*, Gallery Min, Tokyo, 1988. SELECTED EXHIBITIONS: "The Water in the West Project," University of Nevada, Reno, 1991; *Blue Sky, Portland, 1990; "Nature and Culture," The Friends of Photography/Ansel Adams Center, San Francisco, 1990; "Landscape at Risk," Houston Center for Photography, 1989; "Picturing California: A Century of Photographic Genius," The Oakland Museum, 1989; *Silver Image Gallery, Seattle, 1989; *Gallery Min, Tokyo, 1988; "Cross Currents/Cross Country," San Francisco Camerawork and Boston Photographic Resource Center, 1987; "Manifest Destiny—Unsettling America's Family Farmers," The Light Factory, Charlotte, North Carolina, 1987–1989. AWARDS AND GRANTS: Art Matters, Inc., 1990; National Endowment for the Arts Visual Artists' Fellowship, 1988; Ruttenberg Fellowship, The Friends of Photography, 1984; Photographer's Work Grant, Maine Photographic Workshops, 1984; James D. Phelan Award, San Francisco Foundation, 1982. RELATED WORK EXPERIENCE: Co-director of Great Central Valley Project; co-director of California Toxics Project. EDUCATION: MA, San Francisco State University; BA, University of California, Santa Cruz. Currently resides in San Francisco.

TERRY EVANS

SELECTED PUBLICATIONS: *A River Too Far*, Nevada Humanities Committee and University of Nevada Press, 1991; "Beyond Wilderness," *Aperture #120*, Fall 1990, *Atlantic Monthly*, November 1989 and September 1991; *Christian Science Monitor*, December 24, 1986; *New York Times Book Review*, December 7, 1986; **Prairie: Images of Ground and Sky*, University Press of Kansas, 1986; *An Open Land: Photographs of the Midwest, 1952–1982*, Open Lands Project of Chicago, 1983; *Terry Evans/Earl Iversen*, Allen Press, Lawrence, Kansas, 1983; *Life Magazine*, 1978; *Kansas Album*, Kansas Bankers Association, 1977; *No Mountains in the Way*, University of Kansas Museum of Art, Lawrence, 1975. SELECTED EXHIBITIONS: "The Water in the West Project," University of Nevada, Reno, 1991; *"Foreign and Familiar," University of Kansas, 1990; *Salina Art Center, Salina, Kansas, 1989; *Land Institute, Salina, Kansas, 1989; "Women in the Great Plains," Center for Great Plains Studies, Lincoln, Nebraska, 1987; "Exposed and Developed," National Museum of American Art, 1984; "An Open Land," Chicago Art Institute, 1983; "Terry Evans/Earl Iversen," Spencer Museum of Art, University of Kansas, Lawrence, 1983; *Sheldon Memorial Art Gallery, University of Nebraska, Lincoln, 1980. AWARDS AND GRANTS: Mid-America Arts Alliance, Photography Fellowship, 1983; Kansas Committee on the Humanities, 1979, National Endowment for the Arts Photography Survey, 1974. RELATED WORK EXPERIENCE: Member, board of directors of the Land Institute, Salina, Kansas. EDUCATION: BFA, University of Kansas. Currently resides in Salina, Kansas.

PETER GOIN

SELECTED PUBLICATIONS: *Stopping Time: A Rephoto-*

graphic Survey of Lake Tahoe, University of New Mexico Press, 1992; **Nuclear Landscapes*, Johns Hopkins University Press, 1991; *A River Too Far*, Nevada Humanities Committee and University of Nevada Press, 1991; "Nuclear Matters," San Francisco Camerawork, 1991; *Picturing California: A Century of Photographic Genius*, The Oakland Museum, 1989; **Tracing the Line: A Photographic Survey of the Mexican American Border*, limited edition artist's book, 1987; "Old Landscapes Overgrown," *Landscape*, 1982. SELECTED EXHIBITIONS: *"The Land as Witness," Baltimore Museum of Art, 1991; *"Nuclear Matters," University Art Museum, California State University, Long Beach, 1991; "The Water in the West Project," University of Nevada, Reno, 1991; *Cheney-Cowles Museum of Art, Spokane, Washington, 1990; *CEPA Gallery, Buffalo, New York, 1990; "Picturing California: A Century of Photographic Genius," The Oakland Museum, 1989; *Lightwork, Syracuse, New York, 1989; *National Atomic Museum, Albuquerque, New Mexico, 1988; *Visual Studies Workshop, Rochester, New York, 1988; "Tradition and Change: Contemporary American Landscape Photography," Houston Center for Photography, 1988. AWARDS AND GRANTS: National Endowment for the Arts Visual Artists' Fellowship, 1990, 1982; The Sierra Arts Foundation; Nevada State Arts Council Fellowship. RELATED WORK EXPERIENCE: Associate professor of art, University of Nevada, Reno; project director/photographer for the Lake Tahoe Rephotographic Survey. EDUCATION: MFA, University of Iowa; MA, University of Iowa; BA, Hamline University, St. Paul, Minnesota. Currently resides in Reno, Nevada.

WANDA HAMMERBECK

SELECTED PUBLICATIONS: *A River Too Far*, Nevada Humanities Committee and University of Nevada Press, 1991; *ViewCamera Magazine*, June 1991; **Text and Context*, 1980 (portfolio); *Photography: Recent Directions*, DeCordova Museum, Lincoln, Massachusetts, 1980; *Untitled*, The Friends of Photography, 1980; *California Views*, 1979 (portfolio); *Object, Illusion and Reality*, California State University, Fullerton, 1979; *Contemporary California Photography*, San Francisco Camerawork, 1979; **Depositions*, NFS Press, 1978. SELECTED EXHIBITIONS: "The Water in the West Project," University of Nevada, Reno, 1991; "Terra Cognita," San Jose Institute of Contemporary Art, San Jose, 1988; *Museum of Art of the American West, Houston, 1988; "Wanda Hammerbeck and Eikoe Hosoe," Visual Studies Workshop, Rochester, New York, 1988; "Western Spaces," Burden Gallery, New York, 1987; *Etherton Gallery, Tucson, Arizona, 1986; *Carpenter Hochman, Dallas, 1984; *Museum of Photographic Arts, San Diego, 1983; *San Francisco Museum of Modern Art, 1978. AWARDS AND GRANTS: National Endowment for the Arts Visual Artists' Fellowship, 1980, 1979, 1977. EDUCATION: MFA, San Francisco Art Institute; MA, University of North Carolina, Chapel Hill; BA, University of North Carolina, Chapel Hill. Currently resides in Flintridge, California.

MARK KLETT

SELECTED PUBLICATIONS: *A River Too Far*, Nevada Humanities Committee and University of Nevada Press, 1991; *One City/Two Visions*, Bedford Arts, San Francisco,

1990; *Headlands: The Marin Coast at the Golden Gate*, University of New Mexico Press, 1989; *Central Arizona Project Photographic Survey*, Center for Creative Photography, 1986; **Traces of Eden: Travels in the Desert Southwest*, David Godine, 1986; *Second View: The Rephotographic Survey Project*, University of New Mexico Press, 1985. SELECTED EXHIBITIONS: "The Water in the West Project," University of Nevada, Reno, 1991; *Frankel Gallery, San Francisco, 1990; "Visions of the West: Two Views from Two Centuries," Museum of Photographic Arts, San Diego, 1987; *Pace MacGill Gallery, New York, 1987; "Western Spaces," Burden Gallery, New York, 1985; *Art Institute of Chicago, 1984; *"Mark Klett: Searching for Artifacts, Photographs of the Southwest," Los Angeles County Museum of Art, 1984. AWARDS AND GRANTS: Awards in the Visual Arts Fellowship, 1986; National Endowment for the Arts Visual Arts Fellowship, 1984, 1982, 1979; Ferguson Award, The Friends of Photography, 1980. RELATED WORK EXPERIENCE: Chief photographer for the Rephotographic Survey Project; studio manager/photographer for Photographic Collaborative Facility, Arizona State University; geologist and geologist field assistant, U.S. Geological Survey. EDUCATION: MFA, State University of New York, Buffalo (Visual Studies Workshop); BS, St. Lawrence University, New York. Currently resides in Tempe, Arizona.

ELLEN MANCHESTER

SELECTED PUBLICATIONS: Picture editor/researcher, *Colorado: Visions of an American Landscape* by Kenneth Helphand, Colorado Chapter of the American Society of Landscape Architects, the Landscape Architecture Foundation, and Roberts Rinehart Publishers, 1991; co-editor, *Second View: The Rephotographic Survey Project*, University of New Mexico Press, 1984; co-editor, *The Great West: Real/Ideal*, University of Colorado Press, 1977. SELECTED EXHIBITIONS CURATED: "Bravo 20: A National Park Proposal, Photographs and Installation by Richard Misrach," The Friends of Photography, 1990; co-curator, "With the Land," University Art Gallery, Sonoma State University, 1985; co-curator, "The Great West: Real/Ideal," University of Colorado, 1976. RELATED WORK EXPERIENCE: Founder and co-director, Water in the West Project; project director, Rephotographic Survey Project; director of photography, Sun Valley Center for the Arts and Humanities; project advisor/photo historian, Duck Valley (Shoshone-Paiute) Tribal History Project, Idaho; Earth Island Institute, board member since 1981, president, 1987–1990, and secretary, 1990 to present. EDUCATION: MFA, State University of New York, Buffalo (Visual Studies Workshop); BA, Skidmore College. Currently resides in San Francisco.

MARTIN STUPICH

SELECTED PUBLICATIONS: *A River Too Far*, Nevada Humanities Committee and University of Nevada Press, 1991. SELECTED EXHIBITIONS: "The Water in the West Project," University of Nevada, Reno, 1991; *Clarence Kennedy Gallery, Cambridge, Massachusetts, 1989; Houston Center for Photography, 1988; Boston Atheneum, 1988; *The High Museum of Art, Atlanta, 1984; The National Museum of American Art, Washington, D.C., 1984.

AWARDS AND GRANTS: Ucross Foundation Residency Fellowship, Ucross, Wyoming, 1988; Nevada State Council on the Arts Fellowship, 1984; National Endowment for the Arts Photographic Survey Grant, 1979, 1977; Atlanta Bureau of Cultural and International Affairs Special Project Grant, 1981, 1979. RELATED WORK EXPERIENCE: Photographer for Historic American Buildings Survey, the Historic American Engineering Record, and the U.S. Department of the Interior; project director and photographer for NEA Survey Grants in Atlanta, 1977–1980. EDUCATION: MFA, Georgia State University; BFA, Dayton Art Institute, Dayton, Ohio. Currently resides in Dorchester, Massachusetts.

SUGGESTED READINGS

The books and articles cited here are intended as preliminary resources for water, landscape issues, literature, and photography in the American West. Many of the titles have had a strong influence on the work of the participants and on the content and direction of the Water in the West Project.

Abbey, Edward. *Desert Solitaire*. New York: Ballantine Books, 1971.

Adams, Robert. *From the Missouri West: Photographs by Robert Adams*. Millerton, N.Y.: Aperture, 1980.

———. *The New West: Landscapes Along the Colorado Front Range*. Boulder: University of Colorado Press, 1975.

———. *Prairie: Photographs by Robert Adams*. Denver: Denver Art Museum, 1978.

Ashworth, William. *Nor Any Drop to Drink*. New York: Summit Books, 1982.

Austin, Mary. *Land of Little Rain*. New York: Ballantine Books, 1971.

Banham, Reyner. *Scenes in America Deserta*. Salt Lake City: Peregrine Smith Books, 1982.

Bartlett, Richard A. *Great Surveys of the American West*. Norman: University of Oklahoma Press, 1962.

Berry, Wendell. *The Gift of Good Land*. San Francisco: Northpoint Press, 1981.

———. *The Unsettling of America: Culture and Agriculture*. San Francisco: Sierra Club Books, 1977.

Berry, Wendell, Bruce Coleman, and Wes Jackson, eds. *Meeting the Expectations of the Land: Essays in Sustainable Agriculture and Stewardship*. San Francisco: North Point Press, 1984.

Bright, Deborah. "Of Mother Nature and Marlboro Men: An Inquiry into the Cultural Meanings of Landscape Photography." *Exposure* 23(4).

Carvalho, Solomon N. *Incidents of Travel and Adventure in the Far West; With Col. Frémont's Last Expedition Across the Rocky Mountains: Including Three Months' Residence in Utah, and a Perilous Trip Across the Great American Desert to the Pacific, By S. N. Carvalho, Artist to the Expedition*. New York: Derby & Jackson, 1857.

Combs, Barry B. *Westward to Promontory: Building the Union Pacific Across the Plains and Mountains*. Photographs by Andrew J. Russell. New York: Garland Books, 1969.

Conniff, Gregory. *Common Ground: An American Field Guide*. New Haven: Yale University Press, 1985.

Dawson, Robert. *Robert Dawson Photographs*. Introduction by Ellen Manchester. Tokyo: Gallery Min, 1988.

Doig, Ivan. *This House of Sky*. New York: Harcourt Brace Jovanovich, 1978.

Ehrlich, Gretel. *Solace of Open Spaces*. New York: Viking Penguin, 1985.

———. *To Touch the Water*. Boise, Idaho: Ahsahta Press, Boise State University, 1986.

Enyeart, James. *No Mountains in the Way*. Lawrence: University of Kansas Museum of Art, 1975.

Evans, Terry. *Prairie: Images of Ground and Sky*. Introductory essays by Wes Jackson and Gregory Bateson. Lawrence: University Press of Kansas, 1986.

Finkhouse, Joseph, and Mark Crawford, eds. *A River Too Far: The Past and Future of the Arid West*. Photographs by the Water in the West Project. Reno: Nevada Humanities Committee and the University of Nevada Press, 1991.

Fowler, Don D. *The Western Photographs of John K. Hillers*. Washington, D.C.: Smithsonian Institution, 1989.

Fradkin, Philip. *A River No More: The Colorado River and the West*. Tucson: University of Arizona Press, 1984.

Goin, Peter. *Nuclear Landscapes*. Baltimore: Johns Hopkins University Press, 1991.

———. *Stopping Time: A Rephotographic Survey of Lake Tahoe*. Albuquerque: University of New Mexico Press, 1992.

Gottlieb, Robert. *A Life of Its Own: The Politics and Power of Water*. San Diego: Harcourt Brace Jovanovich, 1989.

Guthrie, A. B. *The Big Sky*. Alexandria, Va.: Time-Life Books, 1980.

Hagen, Charles, ed. "Beyond Wilderness." *Aperture #128*. Summer 1990.

Hart, Richard, ed. *That Awesome Space: Human Interaction with the Intermountain Landscape*. Salt Lake City: Westwater Press, 1981.

Haslam, Gerald. *The Great Central Valley Project: Photographs by Robert Dawson and Stephen Johnson*. Berkeley: University of California Press, 1992.

Hayden, Ferdinand Vandiveer. *Annual Reports of the United States Geological and Geographical Surveys of the Territories*. Washington, D.C.: U.S. Government Printing Office, 1868–1883.

———. *Sun Pictures of Rocky Mountain Scenery, with a Description of the Geographical and Geological Features, and Some Account of the Resources of the Great West; Containing Thirty Photographic Views Along the Line of the Pacific Rail Road, from Omaha to Sacramento*. New York: Julius Bien, 1870. (Photographs by A. J. Russell.)

High Country News. *Western Water Made Simple*. Washington, D.C.: Island Press, 1987.

Holborn, Mark, ed. "Western Spaces." *Aperture #98*. Spring 1985.

Houghton, Samuel. *A Trace of Desert Waters: The Great Basin Story*. Glendale, Calif.: Arthur H. Clark Company, 1976.

Jackson, John Brinkerhoff. *The Necessity for Ruins*. Amherst: University of Massachusetts Press, 1980.

Jackson, Wes. *Alters of Unhewn Stone: Science and the Earth*. San Francisco: North Point Press, 1987.

Jackson, William Henry. *Descriptive Catalogue of the Photographs of the United States Geological Survey of the Territories, for the Year 1869 to 1875, Inclusive*. Miscellaneous Publications—No. 5. Washington, D.C.: U.S. Government Printing Office, 1875.

———. *Time Exposure. The Autobiography of William Henry Jackson*. New York: G. P. Putnam's Sons, 1940.

Jussim, Estelle, and Elizabeth Lindquist-Cock. *Landscape as Photograph*. New Haven: Yale University Press, 1985.

Kahrl, William. *Water and Power*. Berkeley: University of California Press, 1982.

Kahrl, William, Stewart Brand, et al. *The California Water Atlas*. Sacramento: California Department of Water Resources, 1979.

Keller, Ulrich. *The Highway as Habitat: A Roy Stryker Documentation, 1943–1955*. Santa Barbara, Calif.: University Art Museum, 1986.

King, Clarence. *Annual Reports of the United States Geological Explorations of the Fortieth Parallel*. Washington, D.C.: U.S. Government Printing Office, 1871–1878.

Kittredge, William. *We Are Not in This Together*. Port Townsend, Wash.: Graywolf Press, 1984.

Kittredge, William, and Annick Smith, eds. *The Last Best Place: A Montana Anthology*. Helena: Montana Historical Society, 1988.

Klett, Mark. *Traces of Eden: Travels in the Desert Southwest*. Essay by Denis Johnson, text by Peter Galassi. Boston: David R. Godine, 1986.

Klett, Mark, Ellen Manchester, and JoAnn Verburg. *Second View: The Rephotographic Survey Project*. Albuquerque: University of New Mexico Press, 1984.

Knack, Martha, and Omer Stewart. *As Long as the River Shall Run: An Ethnohistory of Pyramid Lake Indian Reservation*. Berkeley: University of California Press, 1984.

Limerick, Patricia Nelson. *Desert Passages: Encounters with the American Deserts*. Niwot: University Press of Colorado, 1989.

———. *The Legacy of Conquest: The Unbroken Past of the American West*. New York: W. W. Norton & Company, 1988.

Lopez, Barry. *Arctic Dreams: Imagination and Desire in a Northern Landscape*. New York: Bantam Books, 1987.

McKinney, Whitney. *A History of the Shoshone-Paiutes of the Duck Valley Indian Reservation*. With contributions by E. Richard Hart and Thomas Zeidler. Salt Lake City: Howe Brothers and the Institute of the American West, 1983.

Maclean, Norman. *A River Runs Through It*. Chicago: University of Chicago Press, 1976.

McPhee, John. *Basin and Range*. New York: Farrar Straus Giroux, 1980.

———. *The Control of Nature*. New York: Farrar Straus Giroux, 1989.

Meinig, D. W., ed. *The Interpretation of Ordinary Landscapes: Geographical Essays*. New York: Oxford University Press, 1979.

Metcalf, Paul. *Headlands: The Marin Coast at the Golden Gate. A Photographic and Research Collaboration with Miles DeCoster, Mark Klett, Mike Mandel and Larry Sultan*. Albuquerque: University of New Mexico Press and Headlands Center for the Arts, 1989.

Nabhan, Gary Paul. *The Desert Smells Like Rain*. San Francisco: North Point Press, 1987.

Naef, Weston. *Era of Exploration: The Rise of Photography in the American West 1860–1885*. Boston: New York Graphic Society, 1975.

Nash, Roderick. *Wilderness and the American Mind*. New Haven: Yale University Press, 1967.

Nichols, John. *The Milagro Beanfield War*. New York: Ballantine Books, 1976.

Ostroff, Eugene. *Western Views and Eastern Visions*. Washington, D.C.: Smithsonian Institution, 1981.

Palmer, Tim. *Endangered Rivers and the Conservation Movement*. Berkeley: University of California Press, 1986.

Powell, J. W. *Report on the Lands of the Arid Region*. Facsimile of 1879 edition with introduction by T. H. Watkins. Boston: Harvard Common Press, 1983.

Reisner, Marc. *Cadillac Desert: The American West and Its Disappearing Water*. New York: Viking Penguin, 1986.

Reisner, Marc, and Sarah Bates. *Overtapped Oasis: Reform or Revolution for Western Water*. Washington, D.C.: Island Press, 1990.

Russell, Andrew J. *The Great West Illustrated in a Series of Photographic Views Across the Continent: Taken Along the Line of the Union Pacific Railroad, West from Omaha, Nebraska, vol. 1*. New York: Union Pacific Railroad, 1869.

Sheridan, David. *Desertification of the United States*. Washington, D.C.: Council on Environmental Quality, U.S. Government Printing Office, 1981.

Snyder, Joel. *American Frontiers: The Photographs of Timothy O'Sullivan, 1867–1874*. Millerton, N.Y.: Aperture, 1981.

Stegner, Wallace. *The American West as Living Space*. Ann Arbor: University of Michigan Press, 1987.

———. *Angle of Repose*. New York: Ballantine Books, 1971.

———. *Beyond the Hundredth Meridian: John Wesley Powell and the Second Opening of the West*. Lincoln: University of Nebraska Press, 1953.

Taft, Robert. *Photography and the American Scene. A Social History, 1839–1889*. New York: Macmillan Company, 1938. Reprint: Dover Publications, 1964.

Van Dyke, John. *The Desert*. Salt Lake City: Peregrine Smith Books, 1980.

Wheeler, George M. *Report Upon United States Geographical Surveys West of the One Hundredth Meridian*. 7 vols. Washington, D.C.: U.S. Government Printing Office, 1875–1889.

Worster, Donald. *Rivers of Empire*. New York: Pantheon Books, 1985.

Zube, Ervin H., ed. *Landscapes: Selected Writings of J. B. Jackson*. Amherst: University of Massachusetts Press, 1970.

Zube, Ervin H., and Margaret J. Zube, eds. *Changing Rural Landscapes*. Amherst: University of Massachusetts Press, 1977.

Zwinger, Ann. *Run, River, Run: A Naturalist's Journey Down One of the Great Rivers of the American West*. Tucson: University of Arizona Press, 1975.